Legal Writing from the Top Down

A New Approach to
Better Writing for Lawyers
Second Edition

Timothy Perrin
B.A., LL.B., M.F.A.

Rose Cottage Books
a division of Rose Cottage Media Corp.
W. Kelowna, British Columbia

Canadian Cataloguing in Publication Data

Perrin, Tim, 1949-
    Legal Writing from the Top Down: A New Approach to
    Better writing for Lawyers (2d ed)

Includes bibliographical references.
ISBN 978-0-9812702-0-3

1. Legal composition. 2. Authorship. 3. English language ---
Rhetoric. I. Rose Cottage Books. II. Title

KE265.P47 2010   808'.06634   C90-093517-0
KF250.P47

Originally published in 1990 under the title *Better Writing for Lawyers* by the Law Society of Upper Canada.

Rights Department
Rose Cottage Media Corp.
2966 Sandstone Drive
W. Kelowna, BC V4T 1T2
Canada

ABOUT THE AUTHOR

Timothy Perrin is an award-winning screenwriter, playwright, author and journalist. He has written seven books and contributed to ten more, created several screenplays and TV pilots, as well as authored hundreds of magazine articles. He's interviewed presidents, prime ministers, Nobel laureates, and just plain folk. He's worked for the Canadian Broadcasting Corporation's flagship public affairs program *As It Happens*, been a disk jockey for a Dick Clark-owned radio station, taught creative writing for a college he's never seen and legal research and writing at his old law school. He's visited 20 countries on four continents, 31 of the US states and eight Canadian provinces. Among his adventures have been scuba-diving in the Bahamas, flying sailplanes over the California desert, bike-riding with a nudist club in the Netherlands, patrolling with UN Peacekeepers down the "green line" in Cyprus, and crewing a three-masted square-rigger on the Atlantic. He's an expert on the fire ecology of the giant Sequoias of the Sierra Nevada and on "plain English" legal writing. He has been happily married to his wife Terre for seventeen years—*and* he knows where Buffalo Bill Cody is *really* buried.

In his spare time, he's been known to practice law.

DEDICATION

This book is dedicated to my wife, Terre Perrin, who stuck with me through the worse, the poorer, and the sickness until we got to the good stuff.

TABLE OF CONTENTS

INTRODUCTION

LAWYERS ARE WRITERS

As I write this, my law school class is preparing to gather for a 25-year reunion. We'll talk about how we got broader around the middle and gained a few wrinkles. We'll congratulate the few who've been appointed to the bench or elected law society benchers. We'll show each other pictures of our children and, for some of us, grandchildren. The ones who chose the quiet life of a small town lawyer will look at their classmates who are partners in the big city firms bringing down $1 million or more a year and wonder if they made a mistake. The megafirm partners, in turn, will look at the small towners and envy them their laid back lifestyle, fresh air and ten minute walk to work, a walk where they know most of the folks they pass on the street.

Two-and-a-half decades out of law school, we have all learned a lot more about how little we really know about the law and about the things that make this a fascinating and, at the same time, impossibly frustrating calling.

And we'll find that many of us don't even practice law.

For example, in the last 25 years, I've practiced only nine. The other sixteen, I've made my living as a writer. Most years, I write between 200,000 and 250,000 finished words. That's an average of about 1,000 words per working day — four double-spaced or two single-spaced pages.

I mention that because I wouldn't be surprised if you write more than I do. I know that in the years I have practiced, I certainly churned out more than two to four pages a day. I wrote letters, facta, reports, memos and a dozen other kinds of documents every week and

I'm sure you do too. You may call yourself a lawyer, but in a very real sense, you are a writer.

To do that job well—to communicate on paper, or now on screen—you need to know the fundamentals of writing as well as you understand the basics of contracts. It helps if you have a natural affinity for things grammatical and syntactical but if you don't, you can still cultivate an interest. After all, you don't have to be Eric Clapton to enjoy playing guitar and to do it well. But you do need to pick up the guitar and spend some time getting to know it and what it can do.[1]

It's the same with your writing. Hopefully, as you work you way through this book, you will start to become more sensitive to issues like word usage, structure and clarity. You'll start to notice pieces of writing that work particularly well and be able to figure out why. You'll struggle your way through one that is particularly bad and find yourself reaching for a red pen to see how you would make it better.

In other words, you will start to bring to the written part of your work the same kind of professionalism you already bring to many other parts of it.

WHAT IS "WRITING FROM THE TOP DOWN"

Top-Down analysis is a system of taking a large problem and breaking it into progressively smaller and smaller tasks until you are left with a list of trivial jobs that, when completed, will have solved your large problem.

---

[1] When we did the first edition of this book, my editor questioned my using this reference to Eric Clapton. "It will date quickly," he said. I'm pleased to say that twenty years later, Eric is still making great music, perhaps better than he was in 1990. And if, per chance, you are reading this and *don't* know who Eric Clapton is, get over to iTunes and download some of his solo work and some with Cream and Blind Faith. Trust me on this one.

For instance, if you want to build a house, you start by sketching it out, then working up some detailed drawings and a complete list of materials required. Eventually, it will come down to some workers doing simple things like driving nails or sawing boards—things any one of us could easily do—that, when done in the right order, will build the house.

The biggest building, the most complex spacecraft, the incredible intricacies of computer chips and software are all created using top-down analysis.

And it works with writing tasks, too.

By breaking even the most daunting writing task into a series of much smaller, easier, more manageable tasks, you can relieve your stress and do better work more quickly.

Does it work? Over the last 29 years, I've taught top-down writing to everyone from eighth-graders to university students, law-students to lawyers at some of the top firms in the country. I've taught judges, members of administrative tribunals, trial lawyers, patent lawyers, real estate lawyers and government lawyers. Without exception, those who have applied what I teach in this book have learned to write more easily and more quickly. Several have gone on to teach variations on these techniques to their colleagues or to develop new techniques themselves.

But approaching writing from a top-down perspective does work. It can make your writing go more easily and more quickly. And, most important, it can help your readers. They deserve a break, don't they?

HARD WORK

However, I should warn you that this book is not a panacea. Writing well takes hard work.

That said, it's hardly torture.

In this book, I'm going to teach you some new ways of writing. These techniques are proven, simple and effective. They are the result of studied on just *how* people write and how best to teach writing. Instead of holding up a piece of good writing and saying, "Write like this," I will show you techniques that you can use to make your writing easier, faster and more effective.

Can I guarantee that your writing will get better? Well, as a lawyer, I am reluctant to use a magic word like "guarantee" but I will tell you this: of the hundreds of lawyers who have participated in my *Better Writing for Lawyers* workshops, those who have adopted the techniques you will learn in this book now find their writing easier, faster and better.

In the twenty years since the first edition of this book, I've done a lot of teaching of writing to lawyers, law students, university students, and even junior high school students. Along the way, I've discovered some common problem areas that can be fairly easily addressed. We'll cover those in this edition as well.

HOW THIS BOOK IS ORGANIZED

This book is divided into five parts.

In Part I we talk about some of the problems that underlie the generally poor quality of most lawyers' writing. I also introduce a different way of tackling your writing problems called the "process approach" to writing.

In Part II we'll start looking at the process approach in detail starting with new ways of thinking about what you want to write.

Part III of the book is where I outline how to draft your documents.

In Part IV I'll guide you step-by-step through the revision of your writing.

Finally, in Part V I've included some examples of legal writing I've reviewed over the years along with my comments and rewrites of them. These will give you a better idea of how to apply what you have learned.

HOW TO USE THIS BOOK

You don't have to read this book from front to back to make it work for you. However, if you do follow it through you'll understand a bit more of my thinking and why I have presented the material in the way in which I have.

Don't be afraid to apply what you learn as soon as you learn it. The techniques in this book all work on their own as well as in conjunction with the others. Take what you like and leave the rest. If you're not comfortable with a particular technique, let it go and adopt the others that suit you better. You may later find you're ready for more.

MY PRESUMPTIONS

In writing anything, you have to make a few assumptions about your audience. Here's what I've presumed about you.

In addition to presuming you are a lawyer and that you write a variety of documents, I also presume that you are familiar with the basics of grammar. By that, I mean that when I use a phrase like "predicate adjective" I'm presuming you are with me.

However, I know how long it's been since you may have worked with the academic labels for what you probably do largely out of habit. If you find yourself getting overwhelmed by it all, let me recommend an excellent book called *English Simplified* by Blanche Ellsworth and John A. Higgins.[2] In about 70 pages, Ms Ellsworth and Mr. Higgins manage to cover

---

[2]   Ellsworth, Blanche and John A Higgins, *English Simplified (12th ed)*, Longman, 2009. ISBN 978-0205633296.

everything you need to know about grammar, punctuation, mechanics, word choice, and all those other occasionally difficult subjects. If the answer's not in here, you are asking a truly arcane question and should probably be simplifying your writing entirely.

MY ONE UNBREAKABLE RULE

One more introductory item before we get down to business. In this book, I'm going to lay down a lot of "rules." I commend them to you not because they are laws; they are not prescriptive. Rather, they are *descriptive* of good writing.

Occasionally, a good writer breaks rules for an effect. That's fine provided she knows what she is doing.

The problem is that most people who break the rules of good writing — whether they be punctuation rules, grammatical rules, usage rules, structural rules or what have you — don't have the slightest idea what they are doing.

So that is my only unbreakable rule. You can break any rule I tell you *if*

- you know the rule

- you know you are breaking it and

- you can give a good reason why.

Now, let's get to work.

PART I

THE PROBLEM

Writing is easy. You just jot down ideas as
they occur to you. The jotting is simplicity
itself --- it is the occurring which is difficult.

- Stephen Leacock

CHAPTER 1

WHAT IS WRONG WITH LEGAL WRITING

THE HIT LIST

The catalog of failings of most legal writing is long but several issues are at the core. In the years I have been teaching legal writing workshops, I have seen the same problems crop up again and again: archaic language, wordiness, convoluted sentence structure, lack of organization, rapid changes in direction without any warning to the reader.

All the problems ultimately revolve around the simple fact that the writing of most lawyers fails at its first task: it doesn't communicate easily and clearly.

Clarity

Clarity is at the heart of all good writing. Anything well written is so clear it is transparent. The words disappear and all that remains are the ideas. Think back to any book you have particularly enjoyed. You undoubtedly remember the story and most of the characters but you probably couldn't tell me much about the writer's style, her choice of words, sentence structure or other mechanical issues. That's because you were caught up in the ideas.

But the writing of most lawyers draws intense attention simply because a reader has to concentrate closely if she or he is to hope to understand what the author is saying.

Whenever writing draws attention to itself, it is poor. It's like the scene in a movie where the boom microphone intrudes into the top of the frame. All of a sudden, you're aware that it is all a lie. The illusion is broken. You forget the characters and story and become all too aware of the actors, crew members and director.

Here's a classic example. The following paragraph is from British Columbia's Professional Legal Training Course (PLTC) materials on commercial law:

> *Under s. 67(1), the secured party must make an election with respect to the remedies available to him or her only where the collateral is consumer goods. The secured party may choose to bring an action to recover a judgment against the debtor for the amount of the unpaid debt or other unperformed obligation under the security agreement, or alternatively, the secured party may choose to bring an action to recover a judgment against the debtor for the amount of the unpaid debt or other unperformed obligation under the security agreement, or alternatively, the secured party may choose to enforce his or her security interest in the collateral by seizure (s. 58) or possession (s. 61) or accept a surrender of the goods by the debtor. The remedies are not cumulative. If the secured party proceeds against the collateral by seizure possession or surrender, the debtor's obligations under the security agreement and under any related agreement pertaining to the security agreement (other than a land mortgage executed before July 1, 1973) are extinguished. The obligations of a guarantor or indemnitor of the debtor's obligations are also extinguished.*

That passage contains 188 words in five sentences for an average sentence length of almost 38 words. Two of the five sentences are passive. The passage scores 12.0 on the Flesch-Kincaid Readability Index, meaning you need at least a grade 12 education to understand it. (Most newspapers come in around 6.0. This book scores just over 7.0.)

And, to make matter worse, that paragraph comes after many pages of the same and before many more pages just like it. It's hard to even keep your eyes open when reading such drudge.

But what does it really say?

> **Translation**: In enforcing a security interest on consumer goods, you may seize the goods or sue for the balance due, but not both.

That's it. Twenty-two words.

Now, as it happens, I was a reporter covering the BC Provincial Legislature the day that particular provision was introduced into BC law. The Attorney General at the time was Garde Gardom, a man who you could always count on for a straight answer, and he explained it in just *three* words: "Seize or sue."

Thirty years later I still remember his simple motto. But I've already forgotten the details of the PLTC materials.

Did Gardom leave out the exceptions and the finer points? Of course. But he gave me an idea that I could hold on to and remember. I'm a smart enough lawyer to know that I've got to check the details before I take any action.

But I've always remembered the principle because of the clear, simple way that Garde Gardom explained it: "Seize or sue."

Why?

If legal writing is bad, the question is "Why?"

I expect there are several reasons but the most important are habit, bad example and history.

HABIT

Most of us do things the way we do them because those are the way we have always done them. That doesn't mean those are the best ways, just the most familiar ones.

For example, I have a friend who used to cut the end off a ham before roasting it for the holidays. One day, her husband asked her why. She didn't know other than to say that her mother always did it. So, they asked the mother. She also didn't know why but she said *her* mother had always done it. When they asked grandma, the answer was simple. "Because if I didn't cut off the end," she said, "it wouldn't fit into that undersized baking pan we had."

Since each of us learned to "write" when we were kids and have managed to make it this far in our lives, the habits have obviously worked, at least to some degree. But you wouldn't have picked up this book if you were happy with your old habits.

Shaking habits is always a bit uncomfortable and I can't promise you that the new habits you're going to learn in this book will be as comfortable as the old ones — at least not at first. But soon you'll wear off the rough edges and they'll fit like an old shoe.

BAD EXAMPLES

Another reason the writing of most lawyers is poor is because lawyers see so much bad writing that we start to think it must be right. The sheer volume of garbage most of us read can't help but have an affect on our own output.

But by learning the hallmarks of good writing, you'll soon be able to distinguish the good from the bad.

HISTORY

Finally, to understand why most lawyers write the way they do, it's helpful to know a bit of the history of legal writing, and why the old ways are no longer valid.

Many of the styles lawyers use date to the 16th century, sometimes earlier. This was before the invention of the printing press and long before the invention of the typewriter. Much legal drafting was handled by scriveners who were paid by the word. If a scrivener could use three words where one would do, he got three times as much money. So, quite naturally, scriveners taught themselves to be as wordy as possible.

Of course, today, that's not an issue. The modern style — the one your reader is used to — is short, sharp and to the point.

Another historic anomaly has to do with the spaces between words and with punctuation. Many early Latin manuscripts have absolutely no breaks between words at all. Itwasasifeverythingrantogetherlikethis. As you can imagine, it was hard to read.

Even after copyists began breaking up the words, they used little punctuation. The way you distinguished one idea from the next was in the structure and sequence of words.

Today, however, the rules of punctuation are well established. We don't need to include extra language to make it clear how our ideas are structured.

Yet many lawyers still write that way.

PRECEDENT

Many lawyers use another word for history. They call it "precedent," a word that has almost hallowed meaning within the profession. Many are afraid to move away from the old styles, particularly when it comes to drafting contracts, statutes and regulations. No one wants to end up on the losing end of a malpractice suit and many lawyers think the way to do that is to repeat the mistakes of the past.

It's not. The way to stay out of trouble is to think through what you want to say and then to say it clearly and concisely.

Professor Mark Weisberg of Queens University law school expressed it very well when he said, "It's a question of whether you are in charge of the material or the material is in charge of you."

One of my goals for this book is to show you how to be in charge of your material, how to *know* what you want to say, not just hope you do.

LEGAL WRITING NEED NOT BE BAD

There is nothing inherent in legal writing that forces it to be hard to read. However, lawyers certainly seem to do more than their share of bad writing.

Beswick v. Beswick

But there are also many examples of good legal writing around. Lord Denning of the English Court of Appeal has written some of the best legal prose anywhere. A classic is his decision in *Beswick* v. *Beswick* [1].

> Old Peter Beswick was a coal merchant in Eccles, Lancashire. He had no business premises. All he had was a lorry, scales and weights. He used to take the lorry to the yard of the National Coal Board, where he bagged coal and took it round to his customers in the neighborhood. His nephew, John Joseph Beswick, helped him in the business.
>
> In March 1962, old Peter Beswick and his wife were both over 70. He had had his leg amputated and was not in good health. The nephew was anxious to get ahold of the business before the old man died. So they went to a solicitor, Mr. Ashcroft, who drew up

---

[1]   *Beswick* v. Beswick, [1966] 1 Ch 538 C.A. (England)

an agreement for them. The business was to
be transferred to the nephew; old Peter
Beswick was to be employed in it as a
consultant for the rest of his life at £6 10s a
week. After his death, the nephew was to pay
to his widow an annuity of £5 per week,
which was to come out of the business.

Notice the sentence length. There are 11 sentences in
that passage. They contain a total of 174 words for an
average sentence length of just 15.8 words.

Notice, too, the simplicity of his language.
"Agreement," not "contractual document." "Not in
good health" rather than "suffering from various
debilitating illnesses."

The entire judgment reads like that. Even his
discussion of difficult legal principles is in crisp, short
sentences.

ORGANIZATION

Something that doesn't show in this short passage is
Denning's organization. His judgments were always
well organized. In *Beswick*, as he often did, he
followed that old saw, "Tell them what you are going to
tell them, tell them, then tell them what you told
them."

After laying out the basic facts in the case (remember,
the nephew stopped paying his aunt her annuity and
she sued on her own and as executor of the estate),
Lord Denning doesn't waste any time telling us what
he thinks of the whole situation.

In my opinion, a contract such as this, for the
benefit of widow and children, is binding . . . .
The executor of the dead man can sue to
enforce it on behalf of the widow and
children. The widow and children can join
with the executor as plaintiffs in the action.
If he refuses to sue, they may sue in their

own names joining him as defendant. In this
way, they have a right which can be enforced.
I will now prove this by reference to the
common law, reinforced by equity, and now
by statute.

He then goes on to do just that in sections boldly
headed with the words "The Common Law," "Equity"
and "Statutes." He ends the judgment with a fourth
section under the heading "Conclusion."

One reason Lord Denning has been so influential on
the common law is that you remember Lord Denning's
judgments and forget those of the judges sitting with
him. That's one reason why, even though he's
occasionally been a minority of one, his ideas have
often become accepted twenty years later.

Lang v. I.C.B.C.

Here's another example of good legal writing. This one
comes from one of my students, Ross Tweedale. Ross
is now a Provincial Court Judge but, at the time he
took my class, he was District Registrar for the British
Columbia Supreme Court in Vancouver. One of his
jobs was to handle clients' complaints about the size
of their lawyers' bills. At the time in British Columbia,
we called this "taxing" the bill.

The day before the first session of one of my
workshops, he had written a taxation judgment but
had not yet released it. Here's the beginning of that
judgment.

This party and party taxation resulted from
the settlement of the action by the Plaintiff
and the Third Party on the trial date, October
1, 1984.

The action was commenced as a result of a
motor vehicle accident on August 3, 1982.
The Plaintiff, who had obtained employment
as a strip-tease dancer prior to the accident,

had her employment restricted due to injuries in the accident.

While there is nothing particularly wrong with the writing in this judgment, neither is there anything particularly right with it. It is tedious, wordy and ponderous, rumbling on for another four pages, a total of about 1100 words.

Now take a look at the rewrite of the judgment Ross did after learning some of what you are going to learn in this book. I've included his entire judgment, which runs fewer than 300 words. Note that his first paragraph is only 32 words yet includes all the same information as the two paragraphs above which contain 67.

Darlene Lang worked was a strip-tease dancer. On August 3, 1982, she had a car accident and suffered injuries. These injuries interfered with her work and she sued for damages.

Ten days before trial, the insurance company paid $40,000 into court. Miss Lang refused the $40,000. Then her lawyer had Miss Lang's dance routine videotaped for the trial. Several days after the videotaping, Miss Lang accepted a settlement of $41,000.

Can she recover the $1,000 videotaping cost? I have said "No." This disbursement was neither necessary nor proper. It was incurred extravagantly, negligently and mistakenly. (Any one of the three will do.)

I applied the principles in *Van Daele* [2] to arrive at this result.

Those principles summarized are:

_____

[2]   *Van Daele* v. *Van Daele and London Hotel* (1951) Ltd. (1984), 56 BCLR 178, 45 CPC 166 (BCCA).

1) "The proper test . . . is whether at the time the expense was incurred it was a proper disbursement . . . judged by the situation at the time when the disbursement or expense was incurred." (56 BCLR page 180, McFarlane, J.A.)

2) The principle in *Bogardus* v. *Hill* [3] remains sound: " . . . I think the principle to be acted upon . . . is that all work should be allowed for which a reasonable man, preparing for trial, would feel bound to undertake in order to prove his case."

The lawyer preparing for trial here was directing his mind to settlement. Advising to settle for only $1,000 more confirms this. A "reasonable lawyer" would not have incurred this expense and so I disallowed it.

THE PROBLEM

Se, we see that it is possible to write well in a legal context. The problem is how do you do it? What is the stumbling block between you and the kind of writing you want to do?

With most writing, the problem is not in the putting of words on paper — though that can be a disaster — but in the lack of thinking that has preceded the writing.

The problem is that writing calls on two contradictory skills: it asks you to be both creative and critical. Most of us have little trouble with the critical side. If anything, it is too strong. The problem is in letting our creative sides out, in getting out of the way of what we really can do.

---

[3]   *Bogardus* v. *Hill* (1913), 18 BCR 358 (cited at 56 BCLR, page 181)

Writer and Editor

I like to think that there are two personalities at work inside each of us. There is a creative *writer*, the part of each of us that *knows* how to express itself well. But there is also the restrictive *editor*, the part that says, "No, don't do that! Be careful! You'll look like a fool!"

I'm not saying there's no place for the editor in each of us. In fact, the editor is very important. But we cannot let our editors run us. We have to give the writer room to write *then* let the editor go to work.

The Solution

And that is where we come to the solution. It is only when we organize our writing so that our internal writer can do its job without the interference of our internal editor that we can write well. This book will teach you how to break your writing up into several subtasks, some of which are writer tasks and some of which are editor tasks. That way, you'll be able to be the best writer you can be.

Writing and Thinking

William Safire, who writes the column "On Language" for the New York Times, summarized the central dilemma of writing very well when he said:

> The way you write reflects the way you think, and the way you think is the mark of the kind of person you are.
>
> . . .
>
> You want to fix up your writing, parse your sentences, use the right words? Fine, pick up the little books, learn to avoid the mistakes, revere taut prose and revile tautology. But do not flatter yourself that

you have significantly changed your style.
First, straighten out yourself so that you can
then think straight and soon afterward write
straight. Your writing style is yourself in the
process of thought and the act of writing, and
you cannot buy that in a bookstore or fix it
up in seminar. [4]

Knowing What You Want to Say

So one key to better writing is improving the way you
think about your writing problems. You need to
clearly understand what it is you want to say *before*
you start to write.

Now I've heard many of my students moan, "But I
know what I want to say." I'm sure you often do when
you start writing. But I've reviewed too many samples
of lawyers' writing to buy that you always have it clear
in your mind when you start. Too often, I see the
letter/memo/factum really start on page four, the first
three pages just a warm up exercise through which
I've been forced to plod my way.

So, let's take a look at how we think, how we create
and how we write.

---

[4]   William Safire, "Watch My Style," New York Times, February 9,
       1986. Copyright © 1986, New York Times Company.
       Reprinted by permission.

CHAPTER 2

HOW PEOPLE CREATE

THE CREATIVE PROCESS

In his 1952 book *The Creative Process*,[1] poet Ghiselin collected the works of many creative people on just how they created. He analyzed their comments and recognized a common pattern.

- First, there is a period of hard work during which you put your mind to the problem at hand, gathering information and ideas.

- Second, you wait. During this quiescent period, you don't think you're doing any work on a particular project, but in truth, you subconscious is sorting and analyzing the material you have given it.

- Third comes a moment of inspiration. I know you've had one of these, that moment when the light bulb goes on over your head and suddenly the answer to something pops fully developed into your mind.

- Finally, there's another period of hard work while you get your idea permanently recorded some place.

Creative Recognition

Author Gertrude Stein had this to say about that moment of inspiration, which she calls "creative recognition." She likened it to having a baby.

---

[1]   Brewster Ghiselin, *The Creative Process*, Transformational Book Circle, 2005.

> You cannot go into the womb to form the
> child; it is there and makes itself and comes
> forth whole — and there is it an you have
> made it an have felt it, but it has come
> itself — and that is creative recognition. Of
> course, you have a little more control over
> your writing than that; you have to know
> what you want to get; but when you know
> that, let it take you and if it seems to take
> you off the track, don't hold back, because
> that is perhaps where instinctively you want
> to be and if you hold back and try to be
> always where you have been before, you will
> go dry.

You've probably experienced one or more moments of inspiration like this yourself. I know I have.

For example, several years ago, I was writing an article on science fiction writer Ray Bradbury. I had been to Los Angeles to interview him, reread several of his books and reviewed what the critics had to say. But still, the story wouldn't come.

Finally, one hot night in July, I stepped into the shower to cool off before going to bed. Suddenly, the beginning of the article popped into my head, quickly followed by several hundred more words, already finished as if I had been working on them for weeks. I stayed up until about 2:00 o'clock that morning getting it all down. It later appeared virtually word for word as I first heard it in the shower.

I've heard other writers talk about similar experiences and they all agree: it's almost like dictation.

Of course, writers aren't the only ones to enjoy this kind of inspiration. Dr. Arthur Fontaine, a marine biologist at the University of Victoria, once told me of a similar incident in his research. He had been working with members of the starfish family, animals which have a skeleton made of limestone. However, unlike regular limestone, the limestone secreted by the starfish is porous, filled with million of tiny holes approximately 20 Å in diameter.

Suddenly, one day, without anything to precede it, he realized that the tiny cells that start the regeneration of broken bones were long, sinewy cells about 20 Å in diameter. In a flash, he realized that the material starfish used to make up their skeletons could be used as a substrate for the regeneration of human bone. It was even organically neutral so the host's body wouldn't reject it.

Finally, an example from a completely unrelated field, mathematics. Henri Poincare was a French mathematician. You don't have to know anything about math to appreciate the two instances of creative recognition he enjoyed in this tale.[2]

> For fifteen days I tried to prove that there could not be any functions like those I have since called Fuchsian functions. I was then very ignorant; every day I seated myself at my work table, stayed an hour or two, tried a great number of combinations and reached no results. One evening, contrary to my custom, I drank black coffee and could not sleep. Ideas rose in crowds; I felt them collide until pairs interlocked, so to speak, making a stable combination. By the next morning I had established the existence of a class of Fuchsian functions, those which come from the hypergeometric series; I had only to write out the results, which took but a few hours.

> Then I wanted to represent these functions by the quotient of two series; this idea was perfectly conscious and deliberate. The analogy with elliptic functions guided me. I asked myself what properties these series

---

2   Henri Poincare, "Mathematical Creation," from *The Foundations of Science*. Translated by George Bruce Halsted. First published as "Le Raisonnement Mathématique" in *Science et Méthode*, 1908.

---

must have if they existed, and I succeeded without difficulty in forming these series I have called theta-Fuchsian.

Just at this time I left Caen, where I was then living, to go on a geologic excursion under the auspices of the school of mines. The changes of travel made me forget my mathematical work. Having reached Countances, we entered an omnibus to go some place or other. At the moment when I put my foot on the step, the idea came to me, without anything in my former thoughts seeming to have paved the way or it, that the transformations I had used to define Fuchsian functions were identical with those of non-Euclidean geometry. I did not verify the idea; I should not have had time, as upon taking my seat in the omnibus, I went on with a conversation already commenced, but I felt a perfect certainty. On my return to Caen, for conscience's sake, I verified the result at my leisure.

All of these stories verify the four-step pattern. And, when we understand how something works, we can often put it to work for ourselves

IMPLICATIONS FOR TIME MANAGEMENT

Once we know a bit about the creative process, it begins to have implications for the way we work. In particular, it can help us with time management issues. Here are some tips that will help you make the most out of your time and creativity.

Start Early

First, start each project early enough to allow for incubation time. If you don't give your subconscious time to work, it won't. Some things in life just take their own time. You can't rush a hard boiled egg; you can't force creative recognition.

Incubation is Not Stalling

Second, don't confuse incubation time with stalling. You *need* to put things aside for a while if you are going to do your best work. Again, it's a case of getting out of your own way. Give the job to your subconscious then forget it. You're not stalling. You're waiting for the process to take care of itself.

Carry a Notebook

Third, always carry a notebook for ideas. Creative recognition has its own schedule and it often comes at the most inconvenient times. You have to be ready or those ideas you have waited for will fly off into the ether and you'll miss them. Jot them down when you have them — don't wait.

Schedule Your Time

Fourth, as much as possible, schedule your writing time. For example, if you are a morning person, you might come in at 7:00 each morning, close the door and work on writing projects until 9:00 or 10:00. Train your secretary to fend of would be disruptions during that period and you'll find you get a lot more done. I know this is difficult, but give it a try.

Writing at the same time everyday also tends to train your subconscious that this is its time to express itself. You may find creative recognition waiting for your writing time.

Avoid Deadlines

Fifth, try not to be always working on deadline. Deadline pressure is a common method of overcoming our internal editors and forcing ourselves to do a writing project. It is also highly stressful. What works a lot better is to start thinking about a job several weeks in advance and allow your subconscious to do its job.

Spread the Job Out

Sixth, spread out the time you spend on a particular project. Do it over several days rather than in one hellish session. For example, Spend a hour a day for eight days on a job rather than eight hours at one sitting.

Give It a Rest

Finally, put your writing away for a week or longer then pull it out of the drawer and give it another review. You'll find that your mind will have come to new insights in that period, insights that will often add greatly to your writing.

THE WRITING PROCESS

Understanding the creative process is the just the first step toward becoming a better writer. In the next few chapters, we'll start looking at how we can use our understanding of how we create to improve our writing.

CHAPTER 3

THE PROCESS APPROACH TO WRITING

Twenty years ago, during my undergraduate days at university, my professors in English 1A and 1B would hold up samples of "good" writing and exhort us to "Write like this." Some of us did OK. Many of our friends struggled and — God and a sympathetic professor willing — passed out into the world semi-literate.

Those classes were a joke. We knew it and the professors knew it. Fortunately, some of them cared enough to try to find a better way. Starting in the mid 60's, lead by people like Gordon Rohman at Michigan State, they began to apply the techniques of social science to writing. They dropped the English professor's obsession with *what* writers were writing and started looking carefully at *how* writers wrote.

What they found can help you write more quickly, more easily and more enjoyably. It can also make your writing something worth reading.

THE PROBLEM

Canadian humorist Stephen Leacock summed up the difficulty with writing when he said, "Writing is easy. You just jot down ideas as they occur to you. The jotting is simplicity itself --- it is the occurring which is difficult."

Most of us fall down in the "occurring" stage. How many times have you started a writing task by reaching for the Dictaphone and starting to rattle off the first thing that comes to your mind? If you have, believe me that your writing shows it.

You see, writing calls on two contradictory skills. It asks you to be creative and it insists that you be critical. Only when we exercise both skills in balance — and in turn — can we write well. Too much "creativity" and we may ignore our readers. Too much critical thinking, especially early in a project, and what we write may be far from our best.

THE SOLUTION

While identifying the problem, researchers also found the solution. They discovered that no matter what the genre, successful writers broke writing down into separate tasks, first being creative, then using their critical abilities to hone their creation. The researchers also found that virtually all good writers used a variation of the same three stage process: invention, drafting, revision.

WHAT WE'RE GOING TO COVER

In this book, we'll look at this three-step analysis of writing. It has come to be called the *process approach* to writing because it concentrates on the process of writing, not the product. This chapter provides a general overview of the process approach and in the rest of this book, I'll show you how to apply the process approach to your day to day writing jobs.

In Part II, "Invention," I'll show you how to think about what you want to write, how to get out of your own way and let your creative "writer" do the writing. Part III of the book deals with actually getting your thoughts on paper, the drafting of your document. Finally, in Part IV, we'll look at a systematic way of revising, a system that produces the greatest results for the shortest investment of time.

Now, let's take an overview of each stage in the writing process.

INVENTION

Many writers start a writing job by sitting right down and plunging into battle with a turgid opening, stumbling into a trite middle and on to a hackneyed ending. It doesn't work too well.

Next time, I want you to take time — lots of time — to be creative, to invent. This is the time when you figure out just what it is you have to say. It is also the home of "writer's block" and where most of us get hung up on our writing.

This period of preparing to write is called *invention.* It's a time in which you think about what you are going to say, search out what you already know about a topic, learn more, explore your motives and preconceptions.

Simply put, it's the most important part of the writing process.

Exam Blues

I first ran across invention — though I didn't call it that — in law school. I was not happy with my performance on my very first exam, torts, held on a Friday morning. Instead of spending all weekend studying for contracts on Monday, I spent a few hours reading a book called *Legal Writing; The Strategy of Persuasion* by Norman Brand and John White.[1] One of the things Brand and White recommended was that, on exams, I spend one-third of the time I had allotted to each question just to think about it and to prepare an outline of my answer.

At first, I was nervous about writing an exam that way. After all, my classmates were all madly scribbling away. But I gave it a try and found it worked. My exam answers were shorter, more to the

---

[1]   Norman Brand and John O. White, *Legal Writing; The Strategy of Persuasion*, St. Martin's Press, New York, 1994.

point and much better overall; that first torts exam turned out to be my lowest grade in law school. I also know that my stress level was a lot lower, all because I took the time to *think* about my answer before I started writing.

Letting Go

At first, invention can be hard work. It can be difficult because many of use have been taught that we must always be in control, that there is a "proper" way to do everything and that letting your creative side express itself is most improper.

Invention asks you to take emotional and intellectual chances, to see what is really there. Sometimes you won't end up writing about it, but you do need to know how you really feel as well as what you really know. When all this self-awareness gets too much, just do what I do. When I feel like I'll never be able to finish a particular writing task, I take a deep breath and say to myself, "It's OK to make mistakes. No one will ever know. Mom still loves me." And I start off again.

Let's Make a Deal

During your invention period you must make a deal with yourself. You must let your writer write and get your critical editor to shut up. Sometimes this takes a conscious bargain, one that must be struck again each time your editor starts to interfere. Tell the side of your mind that may be saying "What you are doing is crazy" that it will get full sway during the revision process but for now, it's time to let go and be a bit crazy.

Brain Hemispheres

If you've been following the debate in psychology the last few years about the *hemisphericity* of the brain, some of this may sound familiar. The hemisphericity theory is that the left sides of our brains are linear, logical and critical, the right sides non-linear, analogical and creative. What you want to try to do during invention is foster your right brain while suppressing your left brain.

In Chapter 4, "Starting Off", Chapter 5, "Positive Invention" and Chapter 6, "Focusing and Negative Invention," I'll teach you about several useful invention techniques you can use regularly. Some of these are intentionally unstructured, focusing the power of your right brain. Others are more organized but still help you explore what you already know about a topic, show you where to learn more and, finally, let you decide exactly what it is you want to say about it.

How Much Invention is Enough?

As a rule, spend about one-third to one-half of the time you have set aside for a particular writing task on invention. Invention is the most important part of writing. Drafting and revision are really rather mechanical. Treasure and nourish your invention time and you will improve the quality of your writing substantially.

DRAFTING

If invention is where you spend the most time, drafting is where you spend the least. Many writers spend as little as 10% of their time drafting.

One of the obvious implications of this is that your writing will, of necessity, be shorter. Of course, that is always better. Virtually any piece of writing can be cut.

Don't get hung up on your lead or your conclusion. Just write to get everything down that you want in your letter, opinion, factum or memo. Let your momentum carry you. There is time later to start reorganizing and cleaning up. Now, it doesn't have to be perfect, or even close.

REVISION

The final phase of the writing process is revision. This is the stage where your critical editor is king . . . almost. To make revision work for you, you have to keep a rein on your editor, organizing and controlling your revision.

For example, do you find yourself correcting grammar, spelling and punctuation as soon as you start to edit? Don't. Instead, divide your editing into six or seven separate "passes" through the work. On each pass, look at one aspect of your writing.

The first editing pass is for truth and accuracy. Did the governor really say his opponent has a face like a ferrett? Well, why correct the spelling of ferret (only one t) if you are just going to have to drop the whole sentence anyway?

Take a second run through your piece reorganizing the building blocks. Did you put the discussion of revision before the section on drafting? Now is the time to put them in their places. Do you have a beginning, middle and end? What about transitions? Again, don't worry about the little things. Right now you are moving entire sections, not fiddling with the placement of words.

On your third, more detailed examination of your writing, give a careful look at your paragraph structure. I'll show you how you can analyze your paragraphs and learn how to make them more dynamic and effective.

Fourth, look at each sentence, making sure it does the job you want it to do. I'll show you how to find the critical core of a sentence and how to keep it active and powerful.

The fifth revision is to check you diction and usage. Have you used "less" when you really mean "fewer"? Is it "eldest" or "oldest"? Is there a plain English equivalent for *bona fide*? Do I really need to say "null, void and of no legal force and effect"?

On your last look at your writing, you want to clean up the spelling, punctuation and grammar.

SUMMARY

This part of the book has introduced you to the *process approach* to writing, a system of writing that you can use to make your writing more powerful and effective, that you can use to improve the content of what you write. You've learned a bit about how the mind functions when we're being creative and what that means in terms of time management. I've told you that writing can be divided into a three stage process. First, you must *invent*, finding out what it is you want to say, letting your mind loose and searching for those strange synaptic synergies that only you can produce. Then, you *draft*, getting those thoughts on paper. Finally, you *revise*, only then letting the critical side of your mind influence your decisions.

Now that you know the fundamentals, let's take a look at each phase of the writing process in detail.

PART II

INVENTION

Use the Force, Luke.

- Obi Wan Kenobi

CHAPTER 4

STARTING OFF YOUR INVENTION

LATERAL THINKING

The function of invention is to help you think about your topic. Unfortunately, many of us have trouble breaking our thinking out of old, established ruts.

This chapter explains various invention techniques that are designed to help you break out of your linear thinking patterns into less structured, non-linear lateral thinking patterns. As a result, they are often intentionally unstructured and may take a bit of getting used to. However, if you give them trials, you'll often find them quite useful.

Remember, lawyers are supposed to be creative problem solvers. That means it is your job to come up with the *best* solution to your clients' problem. You can't do that unless you are willing to look not only at solutions that have been used before but at new ones. Those kinds of new solutions are the ones you can often create with these kinds of non-linear thinking tools.

TALK AND WRITE

Perhaps the easiest invention technique is *talk and write*. All you have to do is prevail upon a friend or co-worker to listen for a few moments while you explain your writing project to them. In attempting to make it clear to your listener, you'll find your idea getting clearer in your mind. Usually, ten minutes of talking about a project will focus your thinking quite a bit.

FREEWRITING

Next time you sit down to a writing project, I want you to do this. First, make yourself a promise that *nothing* you produce in the first hour will count. You have permission to make mistakes.

Now, spend just a second thinking about what it is you are writing about. Got it? Now start writing. Write everything that comes to your mind and write as fast as you can. If you are a good typist, use the keyboard. If you find typing slows you down, write by hand.

There is only one rule. You must keep going for ten minutes. You may not pause. You may not go back and correct your spelling or grammar. You must keep going.

If you get off the topic, fine. Just keep writing. Don't worry. There is no way to do this wrong except to stop, slow down, or go back to fix something.

If you can't think of anything to say, repeat the last word over and over or repeat, "I can't think of anything to say." It will start again quickly enough.

After the end of ten minutes, stop. Read over what you have written. Remember, this is not meant to be finished writing or even relevant writing. Try to write a single sentence, no more than four lines long, that sums up the thoughts in what you have written.

Now, use that sentence as the jumping off point for another ten minutes of writing. Then summarize again and another ten minutes of writing.

This process is called "freewriting" and its chief proponent is Peter Elbow of New York State University at Stony Brook, author of *Writing With Power*.[1] It is intentionally unstructured, designed to force your out of your critical mode into your creative mode. With

---

[1]   Peter Elbow, *Writing With Power: Techniques for Mastering the Writing Process*, Oxford University Press, New York, 1998.

the simple goal of writing as fast as possible for ten minutes, your conscious, left brain gets caught up in the immediate task of keeping going while your subconscious, right brain takes over the job of deciding *what* you say. You will be surprised what will come out of your subconscious mind. Sometimes, of course, it will be trivial but often you will find insights that startle you.

Invisible Writing

If you write on a computer, there's a variation on freewriting called *invisible writing* you might want to try. Turn off your monitor or cover the screen with a sheet of paper so you can't see what you're writing. This prevents your critical editor from even seeing your mistakes. Of course, this makes it very hard to be critical. Even if you know you've made a mistake you might as well keep going because you can't see it to fix it.

You don't have to do your freewriting on the computer. If you are more comfortable writing by hand, by all means, do so. Type if you wish. Do your freewriting whichever way allows you to be the least aware of the act of writing so you can let your creative right brain work providing you with good material.

Often, the result of several quick rounds of freewriting will be a clear statement of just what you want to say in what you are writing. It helps to focus your writing.

BRAINSTORMING

Another invention technique — and one of the best and easiest — is brainstorming. This is concentrating on the topic about which you must write then jotting down any idea that pops into your head.

Remember, the key to useful invention is turning off your critical editor and letting your creative writer do the work. In brainstorming, you cannot reject an idea just because it sounds dumb to you. Just jot it down and move on.

You can use brainstorms together with outlining to quickly put a project together. First brainstorm to come up with ideas — perhaps using de Bono's six thinking hats we'll talk about in the next chapter — then do some random sorting and finally pull the brainstorm elements together into an outline.

Brainstorming Practice

If you have a computer, brainstorm on the screen putting each idea on a separate line. If you are working manually, use index cards, putting one idea on each card. You'll see why in a moment.

Now, let's develop a new outline about a real topic. How about *Uses for Cats*? Here's the list of ideas I came up with in about five minutes.

> digging in the flower boxes on the balcony
> Eating
> distracting you from your work
> punching tiny holes in your waterbed
> friend to kids
> none - cats are useless
> friend to strangers
> filling cat box with unmentionables
> keeping up the allergy levels
> taking up the covers on the bed
> Loving
> Petting
> littering the house with dead birds and mice
> keeping your lap warm in winter
> Keeping down the mouse population
> increasing your indebtedness to the vet
> shedding on your best suit
> sitting on your work
> watchcat

Randomly Sorting Your Outline

Logically, the next thing to do would be to impose
some order on the disorder, discarding patently
ridiculous ideas and grouping related ideas together.
But, remember that we're not trying to be logical and
linear but analogical and lateral in our thinking. So
rather than trying to introduce some order to this
outline, let's first introduce some disorder. Let's
scramble the order of the entries and see if the
positioning of completely unrelated ideas next to each
other gives us any new insights.

WORD PROCESSOR SORTS

If you are working on the computer, your word
processing software probably has a sorting ability.
Check your manual to see how to sort your
brainstorm in alphabetical order and into other, less
sensible orders.

For example, I use Microsoft Word as my word
processor. Word has a sorting function that sorts
paragraphs into alphabetic or numeric order.
Normally, it does its sorts starting with the first
character in the paragraph, but I can also make it sort
on the letters in other columns, resulting in different
sequences for my ideas.

Here's a sort that just puts the ideas in alphabetical
order.

> digging in the flower boxes on the balcony
> distracting you from your work
> Eating
> filling cat box with unmentionables
> friend to kids
> friend to strangers
> increasing your indebtedness to the vet
> Keeping down the mouse population
> keeping up the allergy levels
> keeping your lap warm in winter

littering the house with dead birds and mice
Loving
none - cats are useless
Petting
punching tiny holes in your waterbed
shedding on your best suit
sitting on your work
taking up the covers on the bed particularly in
winter
watchcat

But when I sort based on the characters starting in
the fourth column, the sequence is scrambled again.

watchcat
punching tiny holes in your waterbed
shedding on your best suit
none - cats are useless
friend to kids
friend to strangers
digging in the flower boxes on the balcony
Eating
Loving
taking up the covers on the bed particularly in
winter
filling cat box with unmentionables
Keeping down the mouse population
keeping up the allergy levels
keeping your lap warm in winter
increasing your indebtedness to the vet
littering the house with dead birds and mice
Petting
sitting on your work
distracting you from your work

Notice that *watchcat* has moved from the bottom of the
list to the top. We were sorting starting with the
fourth letter and the fourth letter in watchcat is a c,
pretty near the top of the alphabet.

I can randomly reorder my ideas again by sorting on a column starting with the fifth or sixth characters, each time getting a new list.

This ability to sort on second, third and subsequent letters has largely been removed from current word processors, most notably from MS Word, which is a shame. It was in the old DOS versions and it was a very useful tool. Are you listening, Microsoft? Bring it back.

MANUAL MODE

If you did your brainstorming using index cards, you can do the low-tech version of my fancy sorting. You can shuffle the cards and see what order they come up in.

OK, So WHAT DO I DO WITH THESE SORTS?

Good question. You look at them. You read them. Sometimes the juxtaposition of unrelated ideas will trigger off new associations in your mind. See if the reordering of your ideas suggests anything new to you about your topic.

If it doesn't, fine. You've spent a few minutes trying. No one can fault you for that. You can start structuring things now by throwing out some ideas and putting similar ideas together. When you are done you will have the beginnings of an outline.

But if, in the seeming *dis*order, you may spot a peculiar *order* that the rest of us don't see. As a result, your writing will be richer.

Remember, relax and go with the flow.

Remember, brainstorming, like freewriting, has only one real rule: you may not be critical. You must write down any idea, no matter how ridiculous it seems. You can throw ideas away later.

CLUSTERING

In her book *Writing the Natural Way*,[2] Gabriele Lusser Rico suggests a modified form of brainstorming she calls *clustering.*

At the center of a page, put the central concept of your article or story. Now, as you think of sub-concepts, put them around the outside of the central circle, connected by a line. Pretty soon, you will develop a branching structure.

Not everything on a cluster diagram will end up in what you write, but that's fine. Like freewriting, clustering is to help you create. A lot of what you discover may not seem to apply immediately to the project at hand. But the time is not wasted if, among the tailings, you discover a nugget of gold.

The major advantage clustering has over brainstorming is its non-linear nature. A standard brainstorm produces a *list* of ideas. By its nature, a list is linear; it runs down the page. But when those same ideas are spread around the page in a non-linear pattern, they look different and can lead to different conclusions. By clustering or using index cards, you can help yourself break out of linear, logical thinking patterns.

MEDITATION

An often overlooked method of invention is quiet meditation. Spending a few minutes with your eyes closed trying to clear the garbage from your mind will help you to concentrate and will unveil the knowledge you already have.

The kind of meditation I use is really quite easy. Just as in freewriting you tie up your conscious mind with the ridiculous task of writing as fast as you can, in meditation, you tie up your conscious mind with the

---

[2]   Gabriele Lusser Rico, *Writing the Natural Way*, J.P. Tarcher, Inc., Los Angeles, 2000.

ridiculous task of repeating a nonsense word over and over again. That's all.

In many forms of eastern meditation, the nonsense word is called a *mantra*. Many people just use the single syllable *Om*. By quietly repeating the mantra in your mind, making that your focus, you can actually clear your mind of other thoughts. Because your conscious, left brain is busy repeating your mantra, when another thought interposes itself it often comes from your subconscious, creative, right brain.

Somewhat more in the western tradition is the habit of taking a scriptural passage and, in silence and concentration, trying to understand how it applies to your life. You can modify that just a bit by centering your meditation not on a spiritual issue but on the issue in your writing.

Richard Coe says, "Inspiration cannot be forced, but we can 'make space' for it, and meditation is a good way to make that space." [3]

If you are interested in meditation but put off by the "mystical" nature of a lot of it, try reading a book called *The Relaxation Response* [4] by Herbert Benson and Miriam Klipper. It debunks a lot of myth around meditation and provides some simple meditation techniques.

JOURNAL

All writers can benefit from a journal.

Don't confuse a journal with a diary. A diary is a record of what you have done. A journal is a private place where you can share who you are, what you think and, incidentally, what you may have done. Use your journal to jot down the moments of creative

---

[3]   Richard Coe, *Process, Form and Substance: An Advanced Rhetoric*, 2nd ed., John Wiley & Sons, New York, 1981, p. 41.

[4]   Herbert Benson and Miriam Klipper, *The Relaxation Response*, Harper Paperbacks, New York, 2000.

---

inspiration as they come to you. Use it to sum up your thinking on a topic about which you know you are going to have to write. Use it as a storehouse of your ideas, thoughts, hopes and dreams.

You can structure your journal any way you want. Use it as a place to write those letters you could never mail. Try creating a dialogue between two people discussing an issue about which you have to write. Use it for lists of goals, fears, things to do. It's yours to use anyway you find useful.

One tip. If your mind works like mine, if you write in your journal at the same time every day, you mind will get to know that is the time for creative inspiration. Like meditation, it creates space for creativity.

RESEARCH

Research is a fundamental prelude to almost any writing task. Before you can decide what you have to say on a topic, it helps to know what others have said about it already.

For lawyers, research usually means time spent in a library. Don't forget, however, that there are other kinds of research that are often more productive. Can you more effectively research a topic by finding someone who knows about it and interviewing them? And don't be put off by the word "interview." An interview is just a conversation in which you have certain goals in terms of acquiring information. My favorite — and best — interviews have always been the ones where I felt most comfortable with the person I was interviewing.

Of course, sooner or later, on any major writing task, you're going to have to visit a library. It may be just the library in your office where you keep books of interest to your job or it may be a major university research library. Look on it as an adventure, a quest in search of knowledge. Somewhere in that mass of paper is what you need to know. Identify your friends

— they're called librarians — and get them to help you. Most are more than happy to assist you in digging up what you need.

Don't Do Too much too soon

Doing to much research too soon can stifle your creativity. It's easy to get bogged down in what others think and never get in touch with your own ideas. Also, it's too easy to cubbyhole a project too quickly, closing off other, more creative solutions.

As a result, I recommend two rounds of research. Do a quick dip into the literature just to get your bearings then back off. Later, near the end of your invention time, go back and go at it all again but this time in depth.

CHAPTER 5

POSITIVE INVENTION

The invention techniques in this chapter are *positive* invention techniques because they help you create new ideas. They are designed to expand your horizons.

HEURISTIC

If you find yourself wanting a bit more structure to help you generate ideas, try heuristics (from the Greek word *heuriskein,* to find out). These are series of questions that help you explore a topic.

Perhaps the best known heuristic is the journalist's five *W*s: Who? What? When? Where? and Why? By answering those five questions, the same questions a reader will have, you prepare to deliver what you reader expects.

Another heuristic asks you to reconsider the definition of your central concept. How does the dictionary define it? What earlier words did it come from? Answering those kinds of questions helps you understand the relationship of your central idea with those around it by comparing it to other things or asking you to answer questions about its cause and purpose.

There are literally dozens of heuristic available. We'll look at a few in this chapter. Start with these and expand your list as you find new ones.

Burke's Pentad

Kenneth Burke's Pentad, first published in 1945, is a heuristic for exploring human motives. Since so much of the law involves understanding why people act the way they do, it's one you may find particular useful.

At first glance, Burke's Pentad, looks a lot like the journalists five Ws. He asks that we look at the Act (What), Scene (When and Where), Agent (Who), Agency and Purpose (both deal with Why) of events. "Any complete statement about motives will offer some kind of answer to these five questions," says Burke. "What was done [act], When or where it was done [scene], who did it [agent], how he did it [agency] and why [purpose]."

Burke's Pentad reminds us that, when we are writing about the things that people do, we must look at all aspects of their action. To understand human behavior, we can't gloss it over. Human motivation is rarely simple and Burke's Pentad is one of the best methods of investigating it.

To make this heuristic — or any heuristic — work for you, you must spend some time with it. It doesn't work if you see how fast you can read the questions. You've got to stop and think about them. In the case of the pentad, there are subtleties you will want to consider.

ACT — Burke suggests that we not only clarify what happened but that we name the act. Naming it forces us to make a judgment and to put the act into a category.

SCENE — The scene of an act is not just the physical location but the social, political, economic and emotional location. What is the background of the act?

AGENCY — This raises the question How? That can mean the physical or logical tools used. It can mean the media through which a communicative act is made known.

PURPOSE — What goals were achieved, what ends served but the act[s] in question?

AGENT — Most acts have more than one agent. There is a primary actor whom we call the agent. There may also be co-agents, counter-agents or others.

One useful analysis I've been able to transfer from fiction to real life is the standard set of characters you often run into in a film or book. There is always a **hero** who wants something in life. It may be money, fulfillment or happiness. The **nemesis** either wants the same thing or just doesn't want the hero to have it. He or she is not necessarily bad, just in conflict with the hero. The hero's best friend and confidant is called the **reflection**. The reflection shares the hero's goal. In fiction, reflections also tend to die at the beginning of Act III. The fourth standard character is the **romance**. This person loves the hero and wants the hero to achieve his/her goal. To a degree, the romance shares that goal. Almost always, the romance is more emotionally mature than the hero and there comes the scene where he or she says, "I'm leaving. When you figure out what you want to do with your life, give me a call." By the end of the reel, the phone is ringing. Finally, there is the **fifth business**. This is a character whose sole function is to stir things up.

What does this have to do with life? Surprisingly often, this kind of analysis fits real life situations. After all, Shakespeare and his contemporaries did not pull it out of the air. They saw it happening all around them and merely put labels on life. To a large degree, it describes many of our relationships. When you are thinking about the actors in the little drama about which you are writing, these kinds of labels can help you see what is going on.

RATIOS

If you simply answered the questions raised so far, you would learn a lot about the motives of the players in your play but there is more to the Pentad. Burke suggests we look at the interactions of the various elements. Burke calls these *ratios*.

SCENE-ACT

What effect did the scene have on the act? Vancouver is different than Toronto and what goes on here is different than what goes on there just because of the differences in the cities. Vancouver today is different from the Vancouver of ten years ago. An act that might have raised eyebrows then might go unnoticed today.

AGENT-ACT

You will do it differently then I would. The "same" act thus becomes different in different hands. How has the unique nature of the actor affected the act? And how has the act changed the actor?

AGENCY-ACT

What a person can do follows from the tools he or she has available. The house I build in the woods armed only with my handy-dandy Swiss Army knife will be considerably different from one I build in town with all the modern house building tools at hand. Would the people involved have acted differently had they been given different tools: more money, a better education?

PURPOSE-ACT

The purpose to be achieved determines what is to be done. But once the act is chosen does it not also affect what can be accomplished?

ACT-ACT

What acts preceded (and will follow) the act you are investigating? How have they/will they affect this act?

Audience Heuristic

In writing anything from a one page letter to a 3,000 page trilogy, you need to consider your audience. Who is it who will be reading what you write?

Here are some questions you should ask about your audience:

1. Is this audience one person or many? If it is one person, you can rifle your writing right to that reader; if many, you have to use a bit more of a shotgun approach.

2. What does this audience want to learn?

3. What kind of money does this audience make?

4. Is this audience old? Young? What is the average age?

5. What about the social status of my audience? Political philosophy?

6. Does this audience care about religious values?

7. What about the value of education?

8. Which of these three — social, religious or educational values — is most important to my audience?

9. Does this audience expect to read material that follows a certain pattern? What is that pattern? Cause and effect? Thesis, antithesis, synthesis? Storytelling?

10. Do I need to define terms for this audience? Which ones?

11. Does this audience care about its heritage?

12. What could I say that would be most likely to anger this audience? To placate it?

Problem Solving

Often, when we are writing, we are trying to solve a problem. Therefore, our first task is to come up with possible solutions. Peter Elbow, in his book *Writing with Power* [1] offers a series of metaphors that may give you new insight on a problem.

For example, he suggests that your problem may actually be a pump that needs priming. Now, at first, that sounds a bit strange but when Franklin Roosevelt entered the White House in 1933 that was just how he pictured the struggling United States economy. The economy, he thought, is like a pump; it just needs some money to prime it again and everything will be fine. So, he spent and the rest is history.

Here are Elbow's metaphors. Take a moment with each one. Don't rush it.

1. The pump needs priming

2. Defective materials.

3. Too many cooks; a committee designed or executed it.

4. A bribe will do the trick. Bribe whom? With what? [This is one of lawyers' favorites. We call it a "settlement offer."]

5. The problem is that God is angry. At whom? Why? What did that person do to make God angry? [This one can work even if you don't believe in God. Does the other guy?]

6. It's a problem of addiction. Who is addicted to what?

7. The problem has been stated incorrectly. Find two or three ways of stating it differently.

8. The problem comes from bad data. Guess which data are wrong and why?

---

[1]   Peter Elbow, *Writing With Power: Techniques for Mastering the Writing Process*, Oxford University Press, New York, 1981.

9. It's a Gordian knot: stop trying to untie it and cut through it with a sword.

10. The problem is a car that won't start in the winter. What are the things you would do?

11. It's a problem of logic; for example, a is to b as c is to d (A:B::C:D).

12. It looks like a problem, but really everything is fine if you only take the right point of view.

13. Assume the problem has no solution. What is the sensible course of action or strategy that follows from that conclusion?

14. It's a problem in numbers. Try performing the following operations on it: addition, subtraction, multiplication, division, percentages, moving a decimal place.

15. It's just something wrong with digestion: someone ate the wrong thing or has diarrhea, constipation, vomiting.

16. It's a problem of people; incompatible temperaments; struggling for dominance; loving each other but unable to admit it; feeling scared and not admitting it.

17. Outdated design.

18. It's a problem of too little money; or rather too much money.

19. It's sabotage (or self-sabotage).

20. It's a matter of physical sickness. Need for (a) special drug; (b) long recuperation but not much medicine; (c) helping the patient deal with the impossibility of cure.

21. It's mental illness. Needs: (a) shock treatment; (b) talking therapy; (c) group therapy; (d) conditioning therapy; (e) help and support in going through craziness and coming out on the other side; (f) recognition that society is crazy and the patient is sane.

Abstract Concepts

To convey abstract ideas like love, trust and hope, we often need to turn to concrete metaphors. If I say that love is like a spring flower, fragile but able to survive if nurtured, then I can get ideas through to you that I might not be able to convey otherwise. So, when you have to write about abstracts, ask yourself questions that help you put them into concrete terms.

To do this, use all five senses. What does this concept look like? What color is it? What shape? Does it make a sound? What sound? Can it move? How? Does it smell or taste? Like what? Can you touch it? Does it feel like a baby's bottom or a horned toad's head? What size is it? Is it bigger or smaller than other abstractions you can name?

This process of making an abstract concrete may feel strange at first but it is just about the only way I know to get abstracts through to others.

Aristotle's Topoi

One of the first heuristics came from Aristotle and had five basic questions: What is it? What is it like and unlike? What caused it? What can come of it? What has been said about it? Answer those five questions about any topic and you will understand it better and be able to write about it more clearly.

This heuristic [2] is also useful in getting through to the "plain meaning" of a word or term.

DEFINITION

1. How does the dictionary define _____?

2. What earlier words did _____ come from?

---

[2]   Adapted from a heuristic in *Writing* by Gregory and Elizabeth Cowan, Scott Foresman and Company, 1980, p. 34.

3. How has the meaning of _____ changed over the years? Is its meaning different now than it was a hundred years ago?

4. What do I mean by _____?

5. Can _____ be divided? Into what parts?

6. To what group does _____ belong? How does it differ from other things in this group?

7. Can I give some examples of _____?

8. When it _____ most often misunderstood? By whom? Why?

9. What other word have approximately the same meaning as _____? Remember, English has an incredibly rich vocabulary and no two words mean exactly the same thing, but what comes closest?

COMPARISON

1. What is the opposite of _____? What is it most unlike? In what ways are they different?

2. What is most like _____ while still being distinct? In what ways are they alike?

3. To what is _____ superior? What about other meanings of superior (more worthy, physically over, higher in rank, other meanings)? How is it superior?

4. To what is _____ inferior? What about other meanings of inferior (less worthy, under, lower in rank, other meanings)? How is it inferior?

5. To what is _____ similar? How? In what specific ways?

6. From what is _____ different? How? In what specific ways?

RELATIONSHIP

1. What is the result of _____?

2. What are the purposes of _____? Why does _____ exist?

3. Why does _____ happen?

4. What causes _____?

5. What are the effects of _____?

6. What comes before _____? What comes after _____?

TESTIMONY

1. What have I heard people say about _____?

2. What facts or statistics do I have (or can I get) about _____?

3. Have I talked to anyone about _____? What have they said?

4. Quote a parable or well known saying about _____?

5. Do I know a poem about _____?

6. Are there any laws about _____?

7. Do I know any songs about _____?

8. Have I read any books about _____?

9. Have I seen a movie or TV show about _____?

10. Do I want to do any research about _____?

CIRCUMSTANCE

1. Is _____ possible or impossible?

2. What circumstances, qualities or conditions make _____ possible? Which make it impossible?

3. Even if _____ is possible, is it feasible? Why or why not?

4. When did _____ happen previously?

5. Who has done or experienced _____?

6. What can do _____ now?

7. If _____ starts, what makes it end?

8. What would it take for _____ to happen now?

9. What would prevent _____ from happening?

IS IT A MUSEUM?

In one of my classes recently, we had a classic example of this heuristic at work. One of my students was a lawyer for the Ontario Revenue Ministry. Part of his job was to give opinions on whether certain situations meet the statutory requirements for a tax exemption. He'd been asked for an opinion on whether a particular institution was a museum and thus exempt from tax.

The problem was that the particular institution had a definite public relations function. Did that mean it could not be a museum? Right in class, we started to work through the questions in this heuristic.

"How does the dictionary defined *museum*?"   "A building or room in which antiques or other objects of historical or scientific interest are collected and exhibited." [3] Nothing in there about a public relations purpose.

"What makes a *museum* possible?" We could think of no museum that was not funded by someone. None are self-supporting. So, private funding by

---

[3]   *Oxford American Dictionary*, Oxford University Press, New York, 1980.

governments or companies such as the one that runs this "museum" is necessary.

"What have I heard people say about the *museum*?" The lawyer in question had visited this museum and this question helped him remember the remark he had most often overheard: "I didn't know that."

The upshot was that by applying this heuristic, he was able to clarify in his own mind just what a museum is and that this particular institution, in spite of its public relations function, was a true museum.

Checklist for Contracts

Here's a heuristic you can use when you have to draft a contract. It covers the essential elements of any contract.[4]

1. What are the parties and what is their relationship? Notice the question is "what," not "who." This question asks what is the relationship: master/servant, husband/wife, etc?

2. What kind of document do they need? Do they really need a contract at all? Could you get by with something less?

3. If they need a contract, what kind of contract do they need?

4. What is the deal? What is the relationship that needs to be formalized?

    You have to solidify the deal in your own mind. Exactly what are you trying to do? What rights and responsibilities do you seek to create? Since most contracts are business deals, what are the main business points? If you have more than

---

[4]   I adapted this heuristic from "A discourse on disciplined drafting," an article on a lecture by Toronto lawyer John Price. Ontario Lawyers Weekly, February 21, 1986, p. 15. I've added quite a few points of my own but the core is still Price's.

three or four, you probably don't understand the deal.

Prepare an "executive summary" of the deal—no more than two or three pages including the key points and how it will work.

Walk through the deal in your mind looking for hidden potholes. What can possibly go wrong? How would you attack this deal if you were trying to welch on your own contract? Pretend it is your money at stake and do it again.

You should know the deal better than the client; that's what he or she is paying you for. Know it cold.

5. A contract has a beginning, a middle and an end. Does yours? Identify them.

6. What is the effective date? Drafting, typing, signing and delivery can all easily be on different dates. Which of those dates—or which other date—is the date where the contract is to come into effect?

7. Exactly who are the parties? Name them and identify them. This is the time to make sure names are spelled correctly and that corporate names are right.

8. Should you specifically deal with remedies? What are the interests that need protecting? Can cash replace those things? If not, shouldn't the contract specifically address the issue of specific performance vs. damages?

9. Look at *Peevyhouse* v. *Garland Coal* as a classic example where damages were inadequate. That was the Oklahoma case where the Peeveyhouses let Garland Coal strip mine their land on its promise to recontour the land when it was done. The company walked away without fulfilling the contract. Recontouring would have cost about $27,000. The gash in the back yard reduced the

value of the property by $300. The Peevyhouses got the $300, clearly inadequate from their point of view. A lawyer acting for them should have dealt with the issue of specific performance or adequate damages when negotiating their contract.

10. What are the governing law and jurisdiction? They're not always the same

11. Is time really of the essence? If so, have you stated it in such away that the parties clearly understand their obligations. For example, I would draft a "Time is of the essence" clause as, "The parties agree to strictly observe all deadlines in this agreement. They agree that failure to meet a deadline will give the other party the right to rescind the agreement without paying damages." I expect that today you could beat a simple statement that time is of the essence, particularly in a consumer contract.

12. Enurement? Can you come up with one term to cover "heirs, assigns, successors," etc?

13. Assignment? Can both parties assign or just one? What are the limits on assignment?

14. Further Assurance. Do you need a clause saying "We'll do anything necessary to finish off this deal"?

15. Gender Clauses. These days a good idea. [As an experiment, try drafting all your documents in the feminine for a while. It gives you a different perspective on the world.]

16. Notice. How specific need the notice be? Delivered in a certain way? Deemed delivery in a certain number of days if mailed? What about a postal strike? Is notice permissive or mandatory? Price says, "Remember, the first thing anybody who wants to wriggle out of a contract will ask is,

'Is the notice in accordance with the notice clause?'"

17. Representations and warranties. Are oral representations and warranties to be excluded? Can such a clause really be effective anymore? Are there specific warranties in lieu of all others (Remember Federal Express' promise, "Absolutely, positively there in one day or you don't pay.")

18. Arbitration? Don't automatically drop in an arbitration clause. It is not always the cheapest alternative. I've run into a number of problems with mandatory arbitration clauses in my practice. With the small claims limits in many jurisdictions in the tens of thousands of dollars (It's $25,000 where I live) it often makes more sense to proceed in small claims court rather than by arbitrating. You need to think this through and compare the costs. Perhaps this clause should limit costs to the lower of what the party would have received using the less expensive dispute resolution mechanism. Regardless how how you and the other party settle this issue, *think* about it.

THINKING HATS

The inventor of the term "lateral thinking" is Edward de Bono, director of the Cognitive Research Trust and the Center for the Study of Thinking. De Bono has spent his life thinking up ways to help the rest of us think more effectively. So far, he's written more than two dozen books on the subject of thinking, all of which are filled with new insights.

One of his latest book is called *Six Thinking Hats*.[5] He proposes that you adopt six different mind sets by mentally putting on six different colored hats. Each hat stands for a certain way of thinking about a problem. By "putting on the hat" and adopting a

---

[5]   Edward de Bono, *Six Thinking Hats*, Penguin Books, 2000.

certain role, we can think more clearly about the issues at hand. Because we're only "playing a role," there is little ego riding on what we say so we are more free to say what we really want to way.

De Bono likens the process of putting on the six different hats one at a time to that of printing a multicolored map. Each color is not a complete picture by itself. The map must go through the printing press six times each time receiving a new color, until we have the total picture.

Here are the six hats.

White Hat

White is the absence of color. Therefore, when you are wearing the white hat, you think without any biases, emotion or point of view. This is the hat of Joe Friday: "Just the facts, please, m'am."

When you are wearing the white hat, you can only talk about things you know to be true. No conclusions. For instance, it would be fair, while wearing the white hat, to say, "Every swan I have ever seen is white." But watch yourself when you start to say, "All swans are white." You're moving beyond what you actually know to draw a conclusion.

De Bono says, "Imagine a computer that gives the facts and figures for which it is asked. The computer is neutral and objective. It does not offer interpretations or opinions. When wearing the white thinking hat, the thinker should imitate the computer."

Red Hat

The red hat is the hat of emotion. This is the formal channel for things like intuition and hunches. These are important parts of a complete picture of any topic.

As well, it provides a legitimate time to deal with simple emotions: love, hate, mistrust, attraction.

If we don't acknowledge these factors, they will still affect us. Getting them on the table allows us to deal with them. (See the next chapter for some very specific exercises to help you deal with your hidden agenda.)

When wearing the red hat, you never have to justify yourself.

Black Hat

The black hat is, not surprisingly, the hat of pessimism. The black hat thinker points out why something won't work, what could possibly go wrong, why it is a bad idea. But the black hat thinker does not argue this point of view. His job is to simply put those elements on the map to help make a complete picture.

The opposite of the black hat is the optimistic yellow hat. When you are dealing with new ideas, use the yellow hat first or you may beat it to the ground before it has a chance.

Yellow Hat

The person wearing the yellow hat has a sunny disposition. Anything is possible and challenges are merely bumps in an otherwise smooth path. "Yellow hat thinking covers a positive spectrum ranging from the logical and practical at one end to dreams, visions and hopes at the other end," says de Bono.

When you are wearing the yellow hat, you look for the positive aspects of a project: how it will benefit, how a good idea can be made better.

When wearing the yellow hat, think about how to make things work, how to pull something off.

Green Hat

Green is the color of growing things and the green hat is the one to wear when expressing your creative side. When wearing the green hat, you are more concerned with moving along to new ideas than with judging those already at hand.

When you put on the green hat, you are searching for alternatives and new ideas. De Bono suggests lateral thinking techniques such as the "Po envelope." A po envelope is a mental envelope into which you put two randomly selected words. Just open a book, point, and pick two words. Put them side-by-side then ask yourself what they tell you. Because our minds always look for order and structure, your subconscious will find a way to link the two seemingly unrelated ideas. You will find a connection and it will often be useful and interesting.

Blue Hat

The blue sky is over all and when you wear the blue hat, you, too, look down over the entire process. This is the control hat, the hat the controls the use of the other hats.

When you are wearing the blue hat, you monitor the thinking of the other hats, make sure everyone plays by the rules and pull it all together at the end (or at periodic intervals).

PMI

Another of de Bono's techniques involves looking at the plus, minus and interesting aspects of an issue. He calls this a PMI (for Plus, Minus, Interesting).

It's simple. First compile a list of all the positive aspects of a topic. Now put together one with all the problems. Finally, list anything that just strikes you as interesting without being either positive or negative.

The resulting lists will give you a better, explicit look at what you are writing about.

OUTLINING

For most writing jobs, an outline is close to a necessity. For the more technical tasks—drafting contracts, legislation or regulations—it *is* a necessity.

An outline has a natural tendency to be organized and when you are inventing, you don't necessarily want to be organized. So, hold your outline for the end of your invention period. You'll find many parts of it already finished in your other invention materials so you'll just have to pull it together.

Computerized Outlining

If you work on a computer, you will almost undoubtedly find an outlining program a handy tool. Products like *Grandview, Think Tank, Ready, Fact Cruncher* and *Max Think* all allow you to jot down ideas in seemingly random order then to rearrange them into hierarchies easily and quickly.

Now, several of the better word processing programs include integrated outliners so, in essence, the word processing program and the outlining program are one. I use *Microsoft Word* because, among other things, it has a completely integrated outliner. In word processing mode, I have a detailed view of this book, working on the individual paragraphs. By pressing one key, I can step back and see the chapter and section headings, jump quickly through the document to another section or move an entire chapter easily and quickly.

Forget Mrs. Murphy

I have a confession to make. When I was a kid in school, occasionally my teachers would tell us we had to turn in our outlines with something we had written.

I always wrote the outline after the fact, making sure it carefully matched what I had written.

I also recall quite clearly that I had to have my numbering correct: upper case Roman numerals, then upper case letters, Arabic numbers, lower case letters and so on. If I got it messed up, it was points off.

I want you to forget all that. An outline is whatever you find useful for organizing your thinking just before you start drafting. If you choose to do it on the inside of a match cover with—horrors!—not a single Roman numeral to be seen, I won't tell anyone.

CHAPTER 6

FOCUSING AND NEGATIVE INVENTION

This chapter contains some "negative" invention techniques. These are not negative because there is anything wrong. Rather, they help you pare down the size of the task you have created with your positive invention. These help you narrow and focus your thinking, concentrating on what you want to say.

NARROWING THE PROBLEM

Before you start writing, you should narrow the problem on which you must write by asking yourself two critical questions. First, what is the smallest topic with which you can deal? Second, what is the least you can put in this piece of writing?

The two questions are not the same. The first asks you to limit your field of fire, the second asks you to limit the amount of ammunition you use.

Let's go over that again. What is the smallest topic with which you can deal? This asks you to restrict yourself to the questions that really must be answered by this piece of writing. What is the least you can put in this piece of writing? This asks you to deal with those few questions as concisely as possible.

Always ask yourself those two questions explicitly and jot down answers. Remember, you reader doesn't have time to waste. It is your job to make sure that he or she doesn't waste any plowing through your excess verbiage.

Minimal Topic

Normally, a piece of legal writing will have one of only a few purposes:

- To inform a client (letter)

- To create a legal relationship (contract, statute, regulation)

- To deal with another lawyer (letter)

- To persuade a court (factum, brief, submission)

- To state an opinion (opinion letter)

- To record the results of your research (research memo)

Each requires a different approach and each contains different material. What—*exactly*—does this piece of writing need?

Minimum necessary content

One of the major flaw I see in the legal writing I review for my students is that they contain everything *including* the kitchen sink—"just in case." A lawyer who throws in material "just in case" is not doing his or her job. It is your job to know what is *needed*. That's why you're making the big bucks.

For example, a few years ago when I bought a house, my mortgage contained a paragraph that read "And statute labour." That was it, the entire paragraph.

Now, let's start with the fact that it is not a sentence, much less a paragraph. Then let's move on to the fact that there is no statute labour in my home province of British Columbia. Let's continue with the fact that my lawyer at the time—who came from Ontario which still had a *Statute Labour Act*—didn't even know what it was.

If statute labour is that obscure, what the heck was it doing in my mortgage? Oh, I know. "Just in case."

That particular mortgage ran fourteen legal sized pages of barely readable type. At the same time, the Bank of Nova Scotia was redrafting their consumer lending documents and coming up with a residential mortgage about half that length. CitiBank in New York was already using a residential mortgage that was three-and-a-half pages long. Obviously, there is a lot of excess baggage in the mortgage I was handed.

Fortunately, many banks have simplified their mortgage documents but I must admit that rarely—for which read "never"—have I gone through a mortgage line by line with a client. When there's a pile of documents an inch thick for a simple home purchase and the mortgage still runs eight or nine pages of barely intelligible verbiage, I sometime despair.

Anything you writing should have *no more and no less* than what is required. Leaving out something critical is serious. Putting in sections that are not necessary is just as bad; you're leaving more openings for an attack.

UNNECESSARY CONTENT IN ACTION

An example of unnecessary content comes from the opening of a Registrar's judgment from British Columbia Supreme Court Registrar Ross Tweedale.[1]

The endorsement on the writ summarizes the cause of action:

"The Plaintiff's claim against the Defendants, and each of them, is for general and special damages for loss and expense suffered and incurred by the Plaintiff arising out of paint

---

[1]   *Kern Chevrolet Oldsmobile Ltd.* v. *Canadian Pacific Limited*, Registrar's judgment, November 5, 1984. Vancouver Registry Number C824123.

> particle overspray damage to the Plaintiff's
> vehicles and property located at or about 1991
> Lougheed Highway, in the Municipality of Port
> Coquitlam, in the Province of British
> Columbia, which damage occurred on or
> about the 6th day of August, 1981, as a result
> of painting operations negligently carried on
> by the Defendants and or its servants/agents
> or employees which said negligence caused
> paint particles to escape and/or be wind-
> borne to the said premises of the Plaintiff
> causing extensive paint particle overspray
> damage to the Plaintiff's vehicles and property,
> and the Plaintiff claims for costs."

Now there are several things wrong with that
particular recitation of the facts; I'll deal with many of
them later in the book. However, it is obviously so
badly written that Registrar Tweedale does his readers
a real disservice when he quotes it directly. He should
have digested the facts and told them to us in his own
words.

But, for our purposes, the biggest fault with this
version of the facts is that it's simply not relevant.
The case itself has been settled. The only issue before
the registrar is whether the defendant will have to pay
$92,000 of the plaintiff's expenses.

As it turns out, Registrar Tweedale granted the
plaintiff all $92,000 of its claim and the defendant
appealed. In British Columbia Supreme Court,
Justice Patricia Proudfoot dealt with the facts much
more quickly: [2]

> The action involved a claim against the C.P.R.
> for spraying some cars.

Justice Proudfoot obviously had a much better handle
on just what was important *in this particular piece of*

---

[2]   *Kern Chevrolet Oldsmobile Ltd.* v. *Canadian Pacific Limited*,
Chambers judgment, January 30, 1985. Vancouver Registry
Number C824123.

writing. Certainly, in a judgment on the merits of the original case, such a summary of the facts would be inadequate. But, in this taxation judgment, Justice Proudfoot's version is plenty.

IDENTIFY THE CONFLICTS

Writers are iceberg makers. Like an iceberg, 90% of what goes into a piece of writing does not show, but it is there, supporting the writing. Without it, the writing would sink beneath the sea.

Among the unseen things beneath our writing are the conflicts inherent in each piece of work.

Any piece of writing involves conflicts because human activities involve conflicts. For you to do a good job with your writing, you must deal with those conflicts, usually explicitly, occasionally implicitly. However, you can't deal with the conflicts inherent in your writing task if you don't know what they are.

Even if you are going to argue just one side to a question and let a judge do the synthesis, you have to think about the whole picture.

As a rule, conflicts fall into three broad categories: social, emotional and intellectual. In any law practice you will run up against social conflicts all the time. For example, there's the conflict between the right to freedom and the need to protect the public. An emotional conflict arises in your writing when you have to tell the reader something that he or she might not want to hear. How can you minimize that upset? An intellectual conflict exists any time you are asking your reader to accept an idea that may be new or to try any technique that may be untried.

Carefully question yourself about the conflicts inherent in what you want to say. Identifying and resolving these conflicts will lead to a much more sophisticated thesis for your writing. Aristotle said that some truths could be known absolutely, but others only approached. Explicitly identifying and resolving your conflicts is one way of approaching the truth.

CHALLENGING YOUR PRECONCEPTIONS

You've probably heard the story about the father and son who were in a car accident. They were taken to the hospital where the boy required emergency surgery. He was wheeled into the operating room where the surgeon looked at him and said, "I can't operate on this boy. He's my son." What is the relationship between the boy and the surgeon?

Now, I have to admit that the first time I heard that story, I thought the surgeon was the boy's natural father, no, adoptive father, no, step-father. It never occurred to me that the surgeon was the boy's mother. Boy, did I feel dumb when someone finally pointed it out to me.

The story of the surgeon's son is a classic example of a cultural preconception getting in the way of creative thinking.

Seek out your preconceptions. Deal with them *before* you start writing. Only by getting them on the table, acknowledging them and clearing them away can you write clearly and say what you really want to say.

I put preconceptions into three categories, cultural, emotional and legal. But of course, that is only my preconception of the available groups. You may well think of others.

Cultural Preconceptions

Here are some other examples of cultural preconceptions that can get in the way or your writing and creative problem solving.

- **The need to be "in control."** This often interferes with the incubation period creative work needs. It gets in the way of letting go.

- **Playfulness and humor have no place in "serious" work**. A little humor almost always has a place. Remember Ross Tweedale's comment about "It was incurred extravagantly, negligently and mistakenly. (Any one of the three will do.)"

- **Fantasy and reflection mean that you are lazy (or crazy).** I'm in serious trouble if this is true. In fact, I hope that I've shown you that fantasy and reflection are necessary and desirable parts of writing—and hard work.

- **Knowledge must have immediate, practical application to be worthwhile.** If that were true, we could discard 90% of what we learn in life. Most of our lessons are filed away for later use, including some for which we pay dearly in cash and composure.

Emotional Preconceptions

For lawyers, the strongest emotional preconception is the need to play it safe and stick with known solutions. Law is perhaps the most conservative of all the professions. I sometimes think even the church moves more quickly. But if we are to provide creative solutions to client's problems we must occasionally venture into new territory.

Legal Preconceptions

Suppose you have spent $10 on a ticket to go to a play. When you get to the theater, you discover you have lost the ticket. Would you spend another $10 to replace it? Most people in one study say they would not.

But let's rephrase the question a bit. Say you hadn't yet purchased your ticket when you arrived at the theater and discovered you had lost the $10 bill you were going to use to buy the ticket. Would you spend another $10 to buy a ticket? Eighty-eight percent of the people said they would.[3]

So, two questions that were essentially the same got completely different answers. It all depended on how it was phrased.

That applies to legal questions as well.

IS IT A LEGAL PROBLEM?

When a client walks through the door and says, "I've got a problem," you probably presume that it is a legal problem. Perhaps it is not.

Don't presume that the problem is legal because as soon as you do, you limit the possible solutions. Maybe this person needs a doctor, a psychologist, a priest or minister, a dentist, a psychiatrist, a marriage counselor.

We all know that many of the people who come to lawyers for divorces don't really want to end their marriages. They just have run out of imagination. They can't think of any other way out of the mess they feel they are in. Part of your job—as a creative problem solver—is to be their imagination. But you can't do that if your imagination is already mired in the details of a property settlement.

IF LEGAL, WHAT KIND OF LEGAL?

Even if the problem is legitimately legal, what kind of legal problem is it?

The classic example of a legal cubbyhole affecting the solution to a problem is *Donoghue* v. *Stevenson*.[4]

---

[3] Study by Dr. Daniel Kahneman, UC Berkeley, and Dr. Amos Tzersky, Stanford University. Reported in Vancouver Sun, February 27, 1984.

[4] *M'Alister (or Donoghue)* v. *Stevenson*, [1932] A.C. 562 (H.L.)

Remember, that is the case of the dead snail in the bottle of ginger beer. The problem was that the plaintiff had not purchased the ginger beer directly from the bottler. In fact, she had not purchased it at all. A friend had bought it for her. The bottler's defence was simply that Ms. Donoghue had no contract with them so they had no duty to her.

Fortunately for generations of tort lawyers since, Lord Atkin was able to see beyond that narrow legal reasoning and say to himself, "This is not a contracts problem at all but a problem in torts." By characterizing the issue in tort rather than in contract, Lord Atkin was able to break out of the narrow thinking that would have limited the solutions and remedies available to Ms. Donoghue.

LAW OF THE UNITY OF CONTRADICTIONS

The Law of the Unity of Contradictions is a gift to us from our ancestors. I'm afraid I can't claim credit for this one. You can find it mentioned in pre-Socratic Greek philosophy, in the writings of Taoism and in Buddhist literature.

The law says

> If any statement is true, there must be some sense or context in which its contraries are true.

As a corollary,

> If any statement is true, there must be some sense or some context in which it is false.

Applying the law to our theses, the bases of our topic, helps us recognize that they're not absolute, that each thesis has its antithesis.

The Law of the Unity of Contradictions forces us to examine the contrary to each conclusion. It leads us to new perspectives and makes for a deeper understanding and more defensible position.

For example, remember the old saw, "The best place to begin is at the beginning."

Well, sometimes the best place to begin is not at the beginning. Sometimes it is in the middle. The *Iliad* begins in the middle. So does *Oedipus Rex*. In fact, this is such a time-honored literary technique that it has a Latin name, *in media res*, "in the middle of the thing."

Sometimes the best place to begin is at the end. If you begin a piece of writing by stating your thesis or conclusions, you are really beginning at the end.

YOUR AUDIENCE

As the last stage in your invention, refocus on your audience. Once again, think about who will be reading what you are writing. Ask yourself whether you are addressing the concerns of that audience and whether you are considering your audience. The two are not quite the same.

Address the Audience's Concerns

What does your reader want to know? Why is he or she reading this piece of writing? A client wants to know "What should I do?" A judge wants to know "Why should I decide in favour of your client? Give me a reason to lean your way."

Make sure you answer the questions your audience will be asking, not the ones you want to answer.

Consider the Audience

Go back to the audience heuristic. Just who is your audience? Will they buy what you are selling? If not, how can you repackage it to make the sale.

THE NUTSHELL

Toward the end of your invention time, you should be able to summarize your document in a nutshell. The nutshell focuses your document and provides you with a clear statement of where you are heading. Answer these three questions.

What is the **title** of your document? Even if it is not the kind of document that would normally carry a title, give it one anyway.

What is the **purpose** for which you are writing? What are you trying to do with this document? Inform? Persuade? Create obligations and rights? Lay out some facts? Experiment?

Who is your **audience**? If you audience is emotionally threatening, hold off close identification of your audience until after you've drafted.

As the last step in building your nutshell, **summarize** your document in fewer than four sentences.

Example of a Nutshell

Here's an example of a nutshell for an opinion memo on the problem I mentioned in the last chapter, whether a particular institution was a museum.

Title: When is a museum not a museum?

Purpose: To explore and settle the question of whether this particular institution is a "museum" within the meaning of the Act.

Audience: The assessor for the district containing the museum. He's the person who must make the decision on whether or not this institution is to be taxed.

Summary: The institution in question is a museum. Its secondary public relations function does not detract from its primary purpose of education and preservation of history. Its funding is not that much different from other museums.

A concise nutshell like that will keep your writing focused, ensuring that you don't waste you reader's time, wandering around for the answers to those questions.

PART III

DRAFTING

You write with ease to show your breeding,
But easy writing's curst hard reading.

Richard Brinsley Sheridan, *Clio's Protest*,
1819.

CHAPTER 7

THE RED QUEEN SCHOOL OF WRITING

This chapter deals with "drafting" you document. I use the term with some reservations because of the special meaning it has among lawyers. It is not just the act of writing a statute, regulation or contract. In this book, drafting is the act of putting your thoughts on paper for the first time.

RED QUEEN SCHOOL OF DRAFTING

Lewis Carroll had some of the best advice on drafting in Alice in Wonderland. At a point where Alice is trying to tell the Red Queen what has happened, she finds herself confused. The Queen advises, "Start at the beginning, go through to the end and then stop."

Change that just a little. Make it:

> Start at *A* beginning,
> go through to *An* end
> and then stop.

In other words, don't get hung up searching for the perfect opening or the quintessential close. Just start with the part with which you are most comfortable. Work you way out from the center if that is what works best for you. Or start with the close. It doesn't matter.

USING THE NUTSHELL

Remember that the last thing we did during invention was summarize the document in a nutshell: its title, the purpose for which you are writing and the audience and a summary no more than four sentences long. Remember I told you to write them down. Now is the time to take them out. Put them in front of you and use them to keep on course as you draft.

The one exception to this rule is if your audience is threatening, such as the boss in the corner office who tears apart everything you've ever written. In that case, you can hold your audience off until you get to revision.

Three Questions

Do give some consideration to the three critical questions:

- What am I trying to accomplish with this writing?

- To whom am I speaking?

- Why am I writing this?

Answering these three questions—purpose, audience and occasion—will help bring your work into focus. For instance, knowing that I was writing this book for an audience of lawyers who want to become better writers, I am trying to fill it with practical ideas that you can use to improve your writing. Had I been writing it for people who teach writing, I would have been more theoretical and more concerned with telling how to get the ideas in this book across.

The Deal with your critic

If necessary, restrike your deal with your critic. "If you go away now, you can have full sway during revision." Each time your critic starts to interfere, restate the deal. After a while, he/she/it will get the message.

THE OLD ONE, TWO, THREE

There are several points I want you to notice about drafting.

First, you've done a lot of work before ever putting pen to paper (or fingers to keyboard, as the case may be). Up to half the time you set aside for a particular writing task should have been spent on invention. If you had set aside a morning to write a particular letter, you should be starting your drafting about the time you come back from your coffee break.

Second, you don't want to spend too much time on drafting now. Only 10-15% of the time allotted for a particular writing project should go to drafting. Though that sounds difficult, you'll find it's easy when you've done enough invention. You'll know exactly what you want to say and you'll find you have bits and pieces of the document lying around as freewriting, heuristic answers and other fragments you've already developed. And, of course, if you've done an outline, your piece is organized, you know exactly what topics you wish to discuss and you probably have notes on just what to say about them.

Third, accept that you will need to revise. It is impossible to do it right the first time—and if you try, you will not be doing your best.

Justice Martin Taylor of the British Columbia Supreme Court is a former journalist who converted to the law in mid career. He's one of the better writers on the BC bench, and very in touch with *how* he writes. Here's what he had to say about his writing process a few years ago in a speech to a legal writing seminar. [1]

> I have always believed in getting started. I see no merit in clean paper. Rarely have I myself had time to prepare a subject outline or any other sort of scheme. I write. The sentences, paragraphs and pages which emerge are the clay which must be worked on

---

[1] Justice M.R. Taylor, Supreme Court of British Columbia, "Effective Legal Writing: The Lawyer's Role As Technician and Artist In The Written Word", The Advocate, Volume 40, November 1982.

the writer's wheel—expanded, contracted, re-arranged and shaped gradually into a finished object. If I do not know from what direction to approach a problem, I approach it from almost any direction. If I do not know the answer, I start to write what I think is the question. As soon as I see that I have gone wrong—come at it from the wrong direction, asked the wrong question—I know at last what will not do. When you know what is wrong, you are at least that much closer to what is right than you were when you started with a blank sheet.

Inspiration for me seems to be a by-product of the writing process, certainly not a prerequisite to getting started—this is what I mean by the medium of writing creating the message which it conveys.

Justice Taylor is very aware that what he writes the first time through is just a stab, a beginning. He's not trying to do it right, just to get it down. It will have to be "expanded, contracted, re-arranged and shaped gradually into a finished object." In other words, revised.

So get to it. Don't worry about getting just the right word yet. Don't sweat it if you decide you've got the topics in the wrong order. Those are revision issues. At the most, make a note right in your text so you'll be sure to remember to deal with it at the appropriate stage of revision. ***** Set your comments off in a bunch of asterisks or some other unusual characters that will make it stand out in the text as you go back through. *****

TOOLS OF THE TRADE

Things have changed—a lot—since I wrote the first edition of this book. Twenty years ago, computers were just starting to appear on lawyers' desks. In fact, one lawyer who took my course back then told about bringing in her own computer to the office to use in her writing. A few days later, one of the partners dropped into her office, closed the door and told her that her venture into the 20th century was not looked upon with favour by some of the senior partners. They felt it was "too secretarial."

Her reply was simple. "I do a better job on the computer."

"That's just because you haven't learned to use the Dictaphone," he told her.

But she was right.

Writing and speaking are not the same. They use different parts of the brain. Saying "I can write just fine when I dictate" is like saying "I can walk just fine when I swim." Sure, you'll get your exercise, but you won't get anywhere; you'll just go back and forth in the pool. Writer Samuel R. Delany put it very well when he said, "[E]verything I know about writing—and I'm painfully aware how little that actually is—has to do with the difference between written and spoken language." [2]

I've been teaching lawyers how to write better for twenty-five years now and I have *yet* to run into even one that can use a Dictaphone to produce anything better than barely mediocre writing. Yes, I know that Lord Denning dictated some of his best judgments extemporaneously from the bench. I also know that Mikhail Barishnikov can fly across the stage like an angel. That doesn't mean you or I can; I'm always happy when I manage to simply walk across the stage without stumbling.

Dictating is not writing. It's not even drafting. You want to improve you writing? Get rid of your Dictaphone and get a computer. Become a bit "secretarial."

---

[2]   Samuel R. Delany, *The Jewel-Hinged Jaw*, Dragon Press, Elizabethtown, New Jersey, 1977.

If you can't type, it's probably time to learn. We live in a world that is increasingly keyboard and screen oriented. You can despise it, dislike it, and regret it but you can't forget it or ignore it.

Dictaphone madness

If you insist on using a Dictaphone, limit yourself to your first draft. Use it to simply make that first stab at getting things down.

Ask you secretary to prepare everything except final copy in double spacing with extra wide margins. That way, you'll have lots of room to revise. Then ship your marked up copy back for retyping and do the next revision on a clean copy.

PART IV

REVISION

True ease in writing comes from art, not
chance,
As those move easiest who have learned to
dance.
Tis not enough no harshness gives offense;
The sound must seem an echo to the sense.

Alexander Pope, *An Essay on Criticism*, 1711.

CHAPTER 8

INTRODUCTION TO REVISION

SIX REVISIONS

Ernest Hemingway said, "The first draft of anything is shit."

He was right.

That is why all good writers know that *good* writing comes from rewriting, then rewriting again. And again.

And again.

When you rewrite, don't plunge in and start correcting your spelling. Instead, try taking six runs through you work, each time concentrating on a single aspect of it. On the first review, check the truth and accuracy of what you have said. Second, revise the structure; do you have a beginning, a middle and an end? For the third revision, I'll show you how to fix weak paragraphs. The fourth revision deals with your sentences; are they are as powerful as they can be? The fifth time through you document, pay particular attention to your choice of words, the diction. Finally, as a last check, concentrate on the grammar, spelling and punctuation.

THE OVERRIDING CONCERNS

While you are revising, keep two overriding principles in mind:

Clarity

Brevity

Have your Aunt Millie embroider you a sampler with those two words. Hang it on the wall across from where you sit at work. Then, every time you look up, it will remind you of your goals.

Of the two, Clarity is the more important. If you need more words to make your writing clear, then by all means, use them. But, as much as possible, strive to cut out *every word* that is not absolutely necessary.

CLARITY

Clarity is the issue of at the heart of all writing. In their book *A Practical Guide to Legal Writing and Legal Method*, John C. Dernbach and Richard V. Singleton II sum it up well. [1]

> Almost everything you need to know about writing can be summarized in one principle: write to communicate. Since memos are written to predict legal outcomes, you will impress the reader most with good organization, thoughtful analysis and clear writing rather than with rhetorical flourishes, knowledge of Latin or vocabulary. Every last comma in your writing should be inspected, then examined again, to further that principle. Anything you write, no matter how good it sounds should be inspected, then examined again, to further that principle. Anything you write that interferes with the communication of your thoughts, no matter how good it sounds, is wrong.

That simple principal is at the heart of all good writing—even writing that is designed to be intentionally obtuse.

---

[1]   John C. Dernbach and Richard V. Singleton II, *A Practical Guide to Legal Writing and Legal Method*, Fred B. Rothman & Co., Littleton, Colorado, 2009.

Obfuscation

Which brings us to the subject of what to do when you need to muddy the waters. After all, the odds dictate that half the time you are going to have a losing case; perhaps the best thing you can do for your client is throw out so many red herrings that the court will rule in your favour just to get away from the smell.

That's a legitimate objective for a lawyer. However, before you can obfuscate, you've got to know what you are trying to hide. That means that you still have to do your invention so that you are clear on just what it is you *do not* want to say.

And while it may perhaps be occasionally necessary for a trial lawyer to try to blow off a lot of smoke, it's almost always a mistake for a lawyer who spends the day drafting contracts and memos.

Remember my one unbreakable rule. You can break any rule I lay down in this book as long as

- you know the rule

- you know you are breaking it and

- you can give a good reason why.

That applies to my rule about clarity as well. Be prepared to justify yourself. "I didn't know any better," will not beat a malpractice claim.

BREVITY

U.S. President Herbert Hoover is said to have been a stickler about the length of memos. It was standard policy in the Hoover White House that no memo for the boss was to be longer than a single page. Of course, people tried to fudge that rule by making their margins smaller, squeezing more and more onto one page.

One day, the President, tired of trying to make sense out of memos that stretched from sea to shining sea, cryptically told one his aides, "Watch the borders."

The aide, not quite sure what the Chief meant, thought he must know about some threat to the nation. He immediately alerted the FBI, the Coast Guard, the Border Patrol and the Immigration Service. For several weeks, all the guardians of the American frontiers were on alert. Finally, someone finally figured out what was going on.

Now, I don't know if that story is true—I like to believe it is—but it does point out that brevity has been a watchword of good writing for a long time. It's particularly important to your reader.

Keep cutting it in half

Each time you revise, look for words you can cut. Make one goal of each revision to cut your word count in half.

Here's an example of what you can do just keeping an eye out for excess verbiage. Here's the opening four paragraphs from an article by Ken Doolan, a Vancouver Supreme Court Registrar. Here's his original draft.

> In his article for Continuing Legal Education, May, 1982, the Honorable Chief Justice Allan McEachern, Supreme Court of British Columbia, wrote on the subject of "Court Room Decorum, Responsibility and Ethics." He commenced the article by saying:

I do not lightly presume to advise lawyers on conduct in court, courtesy and decorum. These are difficult questions, not capable of easy discussion.

> The learned judge goes on to say that he would not attempt to define good court

manner for that may not be possible. That statement is equally applicable to any attempt to define good Hearing Room manners. I suspect, however, that good manners in the court and Hearing Room are not dissimilar from that minimal social performance generally acceptable in the non-legal world.

You will be aware that a small percentage of counsel who appear before you are addicted to thoughtless and discourteous behavior and, for them, it would be the height of foolishness to embark on a program of reform. While we should not expect the bar to pay homage to ourselves as individuals, we can expect and should insist that they exhibit reasonable respect for the role of the Registrar.

Here's a marked up copy. Text with a line through it is to be deleted. Underlined text is being added. Note that the vast majority of differences between the two version are just words that didn't really need to be there.

In his article for Continuing Legal Education, May, 1982, ~~the Honorable~~ [2] Chief Justice Allan McEachern~~, Supreme Court of British Columbia,~~ [3] wrote on the subject of "Court Room Decorum, Responsibility and Ethics." He **said** ~~commenced the article by saying~~:

I do not lightly presume to advise lawyers on conduct in court, courtesy and decorum. These are difficult questions, not capable of easy discussion.

---

[2] Not necessary outside of formal documents.

[3] The publication for which this article was intended circulates primarily in British Columbia. Believe me, every lawyer in BC knew who Allan McEachern was.

~~The learned judge~~ [4] **Justice McEachern** ~~goes on to say~~ **added** that ~~he would not attempt~~ **it might not be possible** to define good court manners ~~for that may not be possible. That~~. **His** statement ~~is equally applicable~~ **also applies** [5] to ~~any attempt to define good~~ Hearing Room manners. I suspect, ~~however~~, that good manners in **both** the court**room** and Hearing Room [6] are ~~not dissimilar from~~ **about the same as** ~~that minimal social performance generally acceptable~~ **that expected** in the non-legal world.

~~You will be aware that a small percentage of counsel who appear before you are addicted to~~ **Some Lawyers are** thoughtless and discourteous. ~~behavior and, for them, it would be the height of foolishness to embark on a program of reform.~~ **We can't reform them**. ~~While we should not expect the bar to pay homage to ourselves as individuals.~~ **But** we can ~~expect and should~~ insist that they ~~exhibit reasonable~~ respect [7] ~~for~~ the role of the Registrar.

Here's the cleaned up rewrite.

> In his article for Continuing Legal Education, May 1982, Chief Justice Allan McEachern wrote about "Court Room Decorum, Responsibility and Ethics." He said:
>
>> I do not lightly presume to advise lawyers on conduct in court, courtesy and

---

[4]   Again, overly formal for this kind of writing. In an appellate factum, maybe. Not here.

[5]   Rather than using the adjective *applicable* created from the verb *to apply*, why not just use the verb?

[6]   I made it court*room* to parallel the phrase "Hearing Room."

[7]   "Exhibit respect" is turning a perfectly good verb, *to respect*, into a noun. Use the verb.

decorum. These are difficult questions, not capable of easy discussion.

Justice McEachern added that he would not attempt to define good court manners for that may not be possible.

His statements also apply to Hearing Room manners.

I suspect that good manners in both the courtroom and the Hearing Room are about the same as expected in the non-legal world.

Some lawyers are thoughtless and discourteous. We can't reform them. But we can insist that they respect the office of Registrar.

The original contains 168 words, not counting the quote from Justice McEachern. The revision needs only 91 words.

Almost any piece of writing can stand some trimming. Wordiness is the sign of sloppy writing. In an article on how to write an appellate brief, Justice William Bablitch of the Wisconsin Supreme Court put it in terms any lawyer can understand. [8]

An overlong brief communicates exactly the wrong message: insufficient thought, insufficient effort, insufficient grasp of content. Sentences that run on and on, interspersed with numerous commas, paragraphs that dominate an entire page, words that send us scurrying off to our dictionaries . . . eventually my eyes glaze over, roll up in my head, and I begin to emit strange gurgling sounds. These are really not

---

[8]   William A Bablitch, *Writing to Win*, The Compleat Lawyer, Winter 1988.

the reactions you want from a judge you are trying to persuade.

Don't shortchange your readers. Give them less than they expect.

CHAPTER 9

FIRST REVISION

TRUTH AND ACCURACY

The first time you read through your document, concentrate on the truth and accuracy of what you are saying.

TRUE IS NOT ALWAYS ACCURATE

Truth and accuracy are not the same. Something may be true—"He shot at me with a gun!"—but not really accurate—"Well, yes it was a BB gun." So, read through your document and for every statement of fact ask yourself, "Is this true?" "Can I prove it?" "What is my source?" Then also ask yourself, "Even if true, does this statement give an accurate and honest picture?"

Edward de Bono talks about different degrees of truth ranging from "always true" through "usually true, generally true, by and large, more often then not, about half the time, often, sometimes true, occasionally true, been known to happen, never true, cannot be true (contradictory)." [1] Information *may* be valid even though it is less than 100% certain. Just make sure you know how certain it is and just how much you can rely on it.

INTERNAL CONSISTENCY

Also, make sure that your document doesn't contradict itself. It's common, in a long piece of

---

[1]   Edward de Bono, *Six Thinking Hats*, Penguin Books, 2000, p. 49.

writing, to catch yourself near the end saying something the opposite of what you said at the beginning. Watch for it.

WHEN TO CHECK FOR TRUTH AND ACCURACY

There are two times during revision when you could do your check for truth and accuracy: first or last. If you do it last, you may discover that you have spent time polishing a paragraph that is wrong and must ultimately be cut. If you do it first, you may take time verifying facts that eventually get cut for space or aesthetic considerations. Either way, it's a risk. Take your pick.

Actually, it's not a bad idea to do two checks, one at the beginning of revision and one at the end to make sure you haven't added any mistakes.

THE IMPORTANCE OF THE
TRUTH AND ACCURACY CHECK

Is a truth and accuracy check important? Let me give you a quick example from the workshops I teach. One student, a prominent lawyer in a large firm in Toronto, submitted a letter for me to critique. It was an offer to settle a lawsuit for wrongful dismissal. In the second paragraph it offered, "Gross bi-monthly pay in the amount of $1,750.00 less withholding tax at 27% which amounts to a net payment of $1,220.00." The first thing I did was grab a calculator to check the numbers. They're wrong. $1,750 minus 27% is $1,277.50. The lawyer in question had never noticed the mistake because he had not reread the letter for truth and accuracy. At the least, it was an embarrassment; at the most it might jeopardize the settlement negotiations.

We'll get to his mis-use of "bi-monthly" (once every two [bi] months) in Chapter 13.

CHAPTER 10

SECOND REVISION

STRUCTURE

The second time you read through your document, concentrate on its overall structure, its backbone. During this revision, you want to stand back from your writing, take the big view. Does this paragraph really belong at the beginning? This one at the end? Is this paragraph a nice one but ultimately a paragraph that really belongs in another document entirely? Those are the kinds of questions you should ask during structural revision.

THE BASIC STRUCTURE

In reviewing your document's structure, go back to basics. Does your piece have a *beginning,* a *middle* and an *end*? You'd be surprised how often people write documents that don't. Just to make sure, identify those parts of your document and mark where one ends and the next begins.

In the writing business, we call these three parts the *lead,* the *middle* and the *close.*

THE LEAD

The lead is really a special kind of *transition.*

Transitions are passages that let your reader know that there's been a change in person, place, time or topic. "Meanwhile, back at the ranch . . ." is a classic transition. They help your reader make the intellectual switch from one situation to the next.

The lead, as a transition, is to help your reader make the biggest adjustment of all, from the world of his or her reality into the world of what you have written.

Among professional writers, leads are a frequent topic of discussion and a specialized art. That's because it is the lead that determines whether your reader wants to finish what you have written. If you lead is interesting and fulfills its function as a transition, it will encourage the reader to keep reading. If it is dull and leaves more questions outstanding than it answers, your reader will want to put your writing down.

Simplicity is Enough

Leads need not be fancy. They can be as simple as, "Thank you for your letter of last Tuesday in which you asked me if I could visit your office to discuss the proposed merger of your company with Mega Corp International."

What a lead *must do is inform the reader of the people, the place, the time and the topic about which you are writing.*

A lead must also stand on its own. It should not make the reader refer to anything else. It must tell the reader

- what kind of document this is

- why you are writing it

- any other information they need to know to read your document without referring elsewhere.

That's why "Thank you for your letter of February 23," is not adequate as a lead. It forces your reader to return to the files to find the original letter in order to know why you are writing. But adding just a bit to that lead will revive it. "Thank you for your letter of last week in which you asked me to review for you the defences to a charge of possession of ball bearings."

For most writing jobs you will run into in practice, this kind of lead is more than adequate. Just remember that any lead must give the reader just a moment to settle her of his mind onto what you are discussing. It must provide clues on time, place, the people involved and the issues.

Since we so often write in response to something someone else has sent us, by all means refer to it, but don't rely on that reference.

Formal Beginnings

Many legal writing tasks call for certain formalities in their leads. An affidavit, for example, requires that you name the person making the statements and indicate that they are made under oath. However, no one reads these kinds of formal openings and you can still use more effective leads later on in the document when you get to the read issues.

For example, in affidavits or other documents where you are primarily dealing with facts, you might want to try a narrative lead.

Four Types of Narrative Leads

Professional writers use various kinds of leads which you can adapt to your work. Examples are the *anecdote*, the *scene setter*, the *bullet* and the *startling assertion*. These four types of leads are designed to make the reader want to continue reading, to seduce him or her into your document.

Of course, these are not the only kinds of leads. The only absolutes about leads is that they get the reader from where she or he is into your writing. Most of the time, a simple introduction is enough; you hardly need an anecdotal lead on a two page letter. But whenever your document is long enough to possibly put the reader off, try using a little seduction.

THE ANECDOTE

An anecdotal lead is just a short story.

> Old Peter Beswick was a coal merchant in Eccles, Lancashire. He had no business premises. All he had was a lorry, scales and weights. He used to take the lorry to the yard of the National Coal Board, where he bagged coal and took it round to his customers in the neighborhood. His nephew, John Joseph Beswick, helped him in the business.
>
> In March, 1962, old Peter Beswick and his wife were both over 70. He had had his leg amputated and was not in good health. The nephew was anxious to get ahold of the business before the old man died. So they went to a solicitor, Mr. Ashcroft, who drew up an agreement for them. The business was to be transferred to the nephew; old Peter Beswick was to be employed in it as a consultant for the rest of his life at £6 10s a week. After his death, the nephew was to pay to his widow an annuity of £5 per week, which was to come out of the business. [1]

An anecdotal lead usually reveals something about one of the people about whom you are writing. It's a versatile type of lead that can fit on almost any kind of writing because it is just story telling. And, yes, when the topic of your document is a story or a person, it *can* be used on correspondence.

---

[1]   *Beswick* v. *Beswick*, [1966] 1 Ch 538 C.A. (England), Lord Denning.

THE SCENE SETTER

A scene-setter lead, on the other hand, focuses not as much on the people as on the surroundings.

In summer time village cricket is the delight of everyone. Nearly every village has its own cricket field where the young men play and the old men watch. In the village of Lintz in County Durham they have their own ground where they have played these last 70 years. They tend it well. The wicket area is well rolled and mown. The outfield is kept short. It has a good clubhouse for the players and seats for the onlookers. The village teams play there on Saturdays and Sundays. They belong to a league, competing with the neighboring villages. On other evenings after work they practice while the light lasts. Yet now, after these 70 years, a judge of the High Court has ordered that they must not play there anymore. He has issued an injunction to stop them. He has done it at the instance of a newcomer who is no lover of cricket. This newcomer has built, or had built for him, a house on the edge of the cricket ground. No doubt the open space was a selling point. Now he complains that, when a batsman hits a six, the ball has been known to land in his garden or on or near his house. His wife has got so upset about it that they always go out at weekends. They do not go into the garden when cricket is being played. They say that this is intolerable. So they asked the judge to stop the cricket being played. And the judge, much against his will, has felt that he must order the cricket to be stopped; with the consequences, I suppose, that the Lintz Cricket Club will disappear. The cricket ground will be turned to some other use. I expect for more houses or a factory. The young men will turn to other things instead of cricket. The whole village will be poorer. And all this because of a newcomer who has just bought a house there next to the cricket ground.[2]

A scene setter lead is similar to an anecdotal lead in mood but it is not a story. It fills you in on who is there but also tells you about their surroundings.

THE BULLET

A bullet lead is another easy one to remember. It has three examples that illustrate a general point.

> Rex, the Wonder Horse, now 42, has been denied Social Security benefits by the US government.

> Tag, Buster Brown's dog who spent countless years lying under the stinky heels of millions of kids, has been cut off welfare.

> Cheetah, the chimp who saved Tarzan in dozens of jungle epics, is now living on skid row in Los Angeles.

> These are not isolated examples but just three of the tragic cases of animal stars cast aside by society once their usefulness had expired.

Why does a bullet lead always have three examples? Because three seems to work. Try it yourself. Write a bullet lead with four bullets. It doesn't sound right does it? Now try one with two? It's too short. So, three it is. Not for any magical reason; just because it works.

---

[2]   *Miller* v. *Jackson*, [1977] 3 All ER 338 (CA), Lord Denning.

THE STARTLING ASSERTION

A fourth kind of lead, the startling assertion, is designed to surprise your reader so much that he or she will be curious enough to stick with you until hooked.

> *Grazing and Herding News* has learned that Rex the Wonder Horse, throughout his years in Hollywood, has been actively engaged in espionage on behalf of the French film industry. When confronted with the accusation, Rex replied, "Neigh!" and refused to say more without talking to a lawyer.
>
> But the Rex scandal is just a glimmer of what some equine experts suspect is a well organized plot to undermine American values by degrading the quintessentially American film, the western.

THE GENERAL STATEMENT

Most leads end with some kind of *general statement.* This sentence is a transition that tells the reader how the details of this particular lead apply to a larger picture. So, in the first lead about Rex, the Wonder Horse, the general statement tells how Rex and the others are just examples of a larger social malaise. In the startling assertion, it tells how Rex is not the only spy.

The general statement is important. Without it, your reader will wonder how the lead relates to the rest of your document.

Begin At The Beginning?

Remember our modified version of Lewis Carroll's advice,

> Start at *A* beginning,
> go through to *An* end
> and then stop.

That brings me to one of the oldest tricks of leads. Generally I would go along with the old saw that "the best place to begin is at the beginning," but when it comes to leads, sometimes the best place to begin is in the middle or at the end.

BEGIN AT THE END

Whenever you start off by stating your conclusion, you are really beginning at the end. For persuasive writing, this is one of the most useful ways to open. Let you reader know right away just were you are going. Then, with the goal in mind, she or he can follow your argument easily and will end up just where you want.

BEGIN IN THE MIDDLE

When you've got a story to tell, particularly one that is long on woe and misfortune, try beginning in the middle. The *Iliad* begins in the middle. So does *Oedipus Rex*. In fact, starting in the middle is so common and has been around for so long that it has a Latin name, *in media res* ("in the middle of the thing").

Starting in the middle when you are working with facts that are strongly on your side is a way of starting the story—you *are* telling a story—as close to the climax as possible.

Here's an example. Imagine you are in family practice. You arrive at your office at 9:00 Monday morning to find a woman sitting in your waiting room in pajamas, a bathrobe and slippers. She has two small children with her, also in their pj's. When she comes into your office, she is obviously embarrassed and upset. You help her calm down and she tells her story. She has been on the streets since early Sunday morning. Her husband had come home drunk and beaten her. She's finally had enough and wants out.

You now must get an affidavit drawn and get into family court before the end of the day. You need an order for interim custody of the kids, possession of the home and access to money and credit cards. She has already spent two nights sleeping in the back seat of the car. She can't do it again.

Many lawyers I know would draft an affidavit that, after the formalities, begins like this.

> The affiant was married to the respondent on March 1, 1981. They resided at 123 Some Street, in the District of Surrey, the Province of British Columbia.

> The first child of the marriage, Elizabeth Lucille, was born on January 3, 1982.

And so on for six or seven boring, stiltifying pages.

Now, this is a case when there is a story to tell so get in there and tell the story!

> Last Saturday night, my husband came home drunk again. He passed out on the porch steps. I heard him and went out to help him into the house. I supported him enough to get him into bed and was undressing him when he suddenly reached up and grabbed the front of my nightgown. He held on while he swung at me, striking me on the side of the head. "You filthy bitch," he yelled at me. Then he hit me again, knocking me to the floor.

> He staggered from the bed and out into the hall. I heard him go into the room of our son, Michael. Michael is six years old. By the time I got there, Michael was lying on the

floor. I think his father yanked all the covers off the bed, pulling the boy onto the floor.

I ran into the room and shoved my husband as hard as I could. His balance wasn't good and he fell over, stunned. I grabbed Michael's hand, ran into the room of my daughter, Elizabeth, 8, took her hand, grabbed coats and slipper for the three of us, then my purse and keys and fled from the house.

We have spent the weekend living in the car. We have no relatives to whom we can go. We are new in town and have no friends who can take us in.

This is not the first time my husband has beaten me. He has been violent regularly in the nine years of our marriage.

Now, *that* is a lead. I find that when I read that lead to my legal writing classes, things suddenly get very quiet. That's because it is the kind of story that really gets your attention, told with enough detail that a reader can see it happening in his or her mind.

It is also the way your client would probably tell the story to you. It is *her* affidavit, her story. Tell it in *her* language.

One of my students recently mentioned that she had redrafted some of her affidavits in that kind of language and, after reading her evidence, the other side folded. I can't guarantee those kinds of results, but why not give yourself the advantage of the facts when you've got the facts working for you.

THE MIDDLE

After you've polished the lead, move to the middle of your document. When reviewing the middle, make sure that you have included all the details. If you've got an argument to make, make sure you have actually made it and not presumed that your reader would agree. It's a greater sin to skip over details than it is to slow things down a bit to make sure everything necessary is on the page.

Read through your document and check it against this list.

- Are the elements in logical sequence?

- Is each element a small, bite-sized chunk?

- Am I presenting my ideas one at a time?

Reading is a lot like eating. We can take in a tremendous amount if we get it in small bites. However, if we try to swallow the entire roast at once, we'll gag. Don't gag your readers with too much, too fast.

Make Your Point Early

Don't make your reader hang on for the surprise ending. You are not Agatha Christie. Instead, state your conclusions very early in your writing.

> I'm writing in response to your request for our opinion on the validity of the movie option you hold on Tim Perrin's latest blockbuster novel.

> I'm afraid we're convinced it's not any good.

When you state the conclusion right up front, the reader knows where you are going and is more forgiving of your digressions later on.

Table of Contents

While you are closely checking your structure, decide if your document needs a table of contents. For almost anything more than three of four pages long you will want to include a quick list of what is to come in the document and where it can be found. I call this the "table of contents" but don't confuse it with the table of contents of a book.

This table of contents is in prose, not a true table. For example, in this book, you will find it in the introduction under the heading "How this Book is Organized" on page xi.

In a letter or short report, the table of contents could read something like this:

> In your letter you raised several issues. I deal with the first one, whether or not my client is responsible for his actions, starting on the next page of this letter. The second issue, the appropriate penalty, is covered starting on page five.

It's no big deal to you but your harried reader will thank you.

There's a Signpost Up ahead!

While you are checking the structure, make sure you are signposting the turns with transitions. As I mentioned before, the function of a transition is to let your reader know that you have changed mental directions. Whenever the players, the scene, the time or the topic change, you need a transition.

Don't let these scare you. A transition can be as simple as "At the same time as Tim was writing the book in his fashionable office, Jane was struggling with the nine-headed monster in courtroom 34," or as long as an entire chapter.

Whatever you do, don't be subtle. Billy Wilder, the director of such films as *The Apartment* and *Some Like It Hot*, said, "It's alright to be subtle as long as you're obvious about it." You won't impress your reader with a subtle change in direction if the reader misses it. Don't be afraid to say, "That finishes my discussion of the issue of products liability. I now turn to the question of appropriate damages."

HEADINGS AND NUMBERS

One kind of transition tool—one that it is almost impossible to overuse—is the heading. Headings, like the one on this paragraph, serve both as transitions and as navigational aids to the reader later when you document comes in for a repeat reading.

Make your headings informative and make them stand out from the text with boldface, capitalization, underlining or a different typeface.

THE CLOSE

In the close, you can reiterate your main points and sum up.

If possible, close with some kind of resonance with the opening: an allusion, a reference, a metaphor.

> Life today for Rex the Wonder Horse may not be a bed of cherries, but at least he's getting back to those honest roots that made him America's favorite equine star.

Remember that a close has the opposite job of the lead. It is the transition back to reality and the easiest way to do that is to take your reader out the way she or he came in. Resonant closes give your reader a sense of completeness. It's a bit like the nice, solid clomp you like to hear when you slam a car door. If it sounds tinny and lightweight, you don't feel good about the car. A close that just leaves things hanging in the air has the same kind of effect on your reader.

Action List

Much of the time, particularly in letters, the best kind of close is an action list. It specifies who is to do what next and what will happen if it is not done. For example,

> I will go ahead and file the papers on Tuesday. However, if I haven't heard from you by Thursday, March 6, I will drop the action, close the file and send you a final bill.

Or,

> I have done all I can at this point. Now I need you to search through your files and send me copies of all your correspondence with Mr. Doe. When you have done that, I'll be able to start work again. Bear in mind that we are working against a deadline. If we don't file the lawsuit by June 5th, we won't be able to file at all so please work quickly.

EXAMPLE STRUCTURES

Here are some typical structural backbones you will often find in legal writing. Since most of the time you will be dealing with some kind of legal issue, all three of these start with a clear statement of the issue.

Issue - Discussion - Coda

This first structure works well when you are not trying to reach conclusions but merely to explore an area, for example in a general memo for the file on a particular area of law or in a piece for a legal journal.

Start off by stating that issue clearly, then discussing it, then ending by restating the issue.

> You asked me to prepare a memo on the defences available on a charge of possession of ball bearings.

> The history of this offence is fairly recent. The crime was created by Congress in response to the paranoia that developed with

the discovery of the so-called "ball bearing gap" between Soviet and American technology.

. . .

As you can see, there are few defences available against a charge of possession of ball bearings.

Issue/Point - Discussion - Point

You'll find this structure more useful when you are dealing with the facts of a real case. Start off by, again, stating the issue clearly. Then state your conclusion, discuss the issue to show how you got there and end by restating the conclusion.

You asked me to prepare a memo for you on the defences available to our client on a charge of possession of ball bearings. Basically, there are none.

Historically, the courts have been willing to look at three defences in these kinds of cases. However, the recent decision of the Supreme Court in *R*. v. *The Jolly Green Giant* has wiped those out.

. . .

So, as you can see, possession of ball bearings has essentially become an absolute liability offence.

Issue/Summary - Discussion - Conclusion

A third typical structure starts off with the issue, summarizes the discussion quickly, goes into it in greater detail and ends at your conclusion.

You asked me to prepare a memo for you on the defences available to our client on a charge of possession of ball bearings. Basically, there are three: necessity, "I didn't know they were in my pocket" and "What ball bearings?"

The courts have still not decided whether they are ready to recognize the defence of necessity.

. . .

As a result, I suggest we advise our client to take the crown's offer of ten years on Devil's Island and count ourselves lucky that he hasn't implicated us.

RECONSIDER THE AUDIENCE

While you are reading through your document with an eye to structure, it is a good time to check whether you have paid enough attention to your audience. After you've spent all that invention time thinking about audience, it would be a shame to find you have forgotten your reader in the drafting.

Go back to the two questions you addressed at the end of your invention. Have I addressed the concerns of my audience? Have I considered my audience? Again, those two are similar but different questions.

"Have I addressed the concerns of my audience?" could be restated, "Does my document answer my reader's questions?" I often find that in a letter to a client a lawyer will detail his or her trip to the library and what the law says about the client's problem. What these lawyers often forget to do is what they are being paid for: tell the client what he or she should do. That is why the client is reading the letter: for advice. Those lawyers don't deliver because they haven't addressed the concerns of their audience.

Considering your audience is a bit different. This is an appreciation of the person or persons who will be reading your document. Is you reader a formal person, someone who expects old fashioned courtesies rather than modern breeziness? Well then, you'd better drop the line that says, "That's about it," and replace it with "I trust this meets your needs."

CHAPTER 11

THIRD REVISION

PARAGRAPHS

On your third revision of your document, pay particular attention to your paragraphs.

The paragraph is the basic unit of writing yet many writers, even experienced ones, are unclear on just what a paragraph is and how it functions.

It works like this.

PARAGRAPH ANALYSIS

In English, we discuss ideas by moving from general concepts to more specific ones, much the way outlines are arranged. A paragraph, as the essential unit of thought in English, works the same way. It consists of a general statement, the *topic sentence,* followed by a group of ideas (sentences) all related to the general statement. That much you probably already knew.

But there is a system of analyzing paragraphs developed by Prof. Francis Christensen.[1] In Christensen's analysis, we label the most general statement in the paragraph, the topic sentence, with a 1. Ideas (sentences) one level of generality more specific we label 2. The next level down, ideas even more specific, we label 3 and so on.

When you "chart" a paragraph this way, you get an instant picture of its structure. If you find it difficult

---

[1]   Francis Christensen, "A Generative Rhetoric of the Paragraph" in *Contemporary Rhetoric,* Conceptual Background With Readings, edited by W. Ross Winterowd, Harcourt Brace Jovanovich, 1975.

to chart a paragraph, it's usually a good sign that there are big problems with the paragraph.

Let me give you a few examples.

Here's a paragraph that is an example of a *subordinate* paragraph structure. Each sentence in the paragraph is more specific than the previous.

1. In English, we discuss ideas by moving from general concepts to more specific ones, much the way outlines are arranged.

    2. A paragraph, as the essential unit of thought in English, works the same way.

        3. It consists of a general statement, the *topic sentence*, followed by a group of ideas (sentences) all related to the general statement.

            4. That much you probably already knew.

Notice how each sentence relates to the topic sentence through the previous sentence. Remove any sentence from the sequence and it won't make as much sense.

Now here is an example of the other main paragraph structure, a *coordinate* paragraph.

1. Whatever you do, don't be subtle.

    2. I think it was Billy Wilder, the director of such films as *The Apartment* and *Some Like It Hot* who said, "It's alright to be subtle as long as you're obvious about it."

    2. You won't impress your reader with a subtle change in direction if the reader misses it.

    2. Don't be afraid to say, "That finishes my discussion of the issue of products liability. I

now turn to the question of appropriate damages."

Notice that each of the sentences labeled "2" could directly follow the first; they could go in almost any order. That is one mark of a coordinate structure.

You certainly don't need to analyze each of your paragraphs like this; it would take much too long. However, when you are having trouble with a paragraph, perhaps wondering whether or not to start a new paragraph at a particular place, this method can help you.

Examples

Of course, life, and writing, are not that simple. Usually paragraphs have some kind of combined structure. Here are some more examples of paragraphs analyzed using Christensen's system. They'll give you a better idea of how paragraphs fit together.

COORDINATE STRUCTURE

1. This is the essence of the religious spirit—the sense of power, beauty, greatness, truth infinitely beyond one's own reach, but infinitely to be aspired to.

    2. It invests men with pride in a purpose and with humility in accomplishment.

    2. It is the source of all true tolerance, for in its light all men see other men as they see themselves, as being capable of being more than they are, and yet falling short, inevitably, of what they can imagine human opportunities to be.

    2. It is the supporter of human dignity and pride and the dissolver of vanity.

2. And it is the very creator of the scientific spirit; for without the aspiration to understand and control the miracle of life, no man would have sweated in a laboratory or tortured his brain in the exquisite search after truth.[2]

SUBORDINATE STRUCTURE

1. The process of learning is essential our lives.

2. All higher animals seek it deliberately.

3. They are inquisitive and they experiment.

4. An experiment is a sort of harmless trial run of some action which we shall have to make in the real world; and this, whether it is made in the laboratory by scientists or by fox-cubs outside their earth.

5. The scientist experiments and the cub plays; both are learning to correct their errors of judgment in a setting in which errors are not fatal.

6. Perhaps this is what gives them both their air of happiness and freedom in these activities.[3]

---

[2] Dorothy Thompson.

[3] Jacob Bronowski, *The Common Sense of Science*, Harvard University Press, 1952.

COMBINED STRUCTURE BASED ON A COORDINATE STRUCTURE

1. This is a point so frequently not understood that it needs some dwelling on.

    2. Consider how difficult it is to find a tenable argument that thrown, say, is intrinsically better than throwed.

        3. We can hardly say that the simple sound it better.

            4. For if it were, we would presumable also prefer rown to rowed, hown to hoed, strown to stowed, and we don't.

        3. Now can we argue convincingly that throwed should be avoided because it did not occur in earlier English.

            4. Many forms which occurred in earlier English cannot now be used.

                5. As we mentioned earlier, holp used to be the past tense form of help; helped was incorrect.

                5. But we could not now say, "He holp me a good deal."

    2. As for "me and Jim," the statement that I should be used in the subject position begs the question.

        3. One can ask why I should be the subject form and to this there is no answer.

            4. As a matter of fact, you was at one time the object form of the second

personal plural, ye being the subject form.

4. But no one objects now to a sentence like "You were there." [4]

COMBINED STRUCTURE BASED ON A SUBORDINATE STRUCTURE

1. The purpose of science is to describe the world in an orderly scheme or language which will help us look ahead.

2. We want to forecast what we can of the future behavior of the world, particularly we want to forecast how it would behave under several alternative actions of our own between which we are usually trying to choose.

3. This is a very limited purpose.

4. It has nothing whatever to do with bold generalizations about the universal working of cause and effect.

4. It has nothing to do with cause and effect at all, or with any other special mechanism.

4. Nothing in this purpose, which is to order the world as an aid to decision and action, implies that the order must be of one kind rather than other.

5. The order is what we find to work, conveniently and instructively.

---

[4]   Paul Roberts.

5. It is not something we stipulate;
    it is not something we can
    dogmatize about.

5. It is what we find; it is what we
    find useful.[5]

Exercise

Now, try it yourself. Here's a fairly complicated
paragraph that you saw earlier in this book. Try
analyzing it using Christensen's system. One clue:
this is a trick paragraph.

In summer time village cricket is the delight
of everyone. Nearly every village has its own
cricket field where the young men play and
the old men watch. In the village of Lintz in
County Durham they have their own ground
where they have played these last 70 years.
They tend it well. The wicket area is well
rolled and mown. The outfield is kept short.
It has a good clubhouse for the players and
seats for the onlookers. The village teams
play there on Saturdays and Sundays. They
belong to a league, competing with the
neighboring villages. On other evenings after
work they practice while the light lasts. Yet
now, after these 70 years, a judge of the High
Court has ordered that they must not play
there anymore. He has issued an injunction
to stop them. He has done it at the instance
of a newcomer who is no lover of cricket.
This newcomer has built, or had built for him
a house on the edge of the cricket ground.
No doubt the open space was a selling point.
Now he complains that, when a batsman hits
a six, the ball has been known to land in his
garden or on or near his house. His wife has
got so upset about it that they always go out

[5]   Jacob Bronowski, *The Common Sense of Science*, Harvard
University Press, 1952.

at weekends. They do not go into the garden when cricket is being played. They say that this is intolerable. So they asked the judge to stop the cricket being played. And the judge, much against his will, has felt that he must order the cricket to be stopped; with the consequences, I suppose, that the Lintz Cricket Club will disappear. The cricket ground will be turned to some other use. I expect for more houses or a factory. The young men will turn to other things instead of cricket. The whole village will be poorer. And all this because of a newcomer who has just bought a house there next to the cricket ground.[6]

THE ANSWER

Here's one answer. This isn't a science so there are certainly possible variations on this analysis. However, I think this fairly dissects this particular paragraph.

The trick, by the way, was that Lord Denning really had two paragraphs here.

1.   In summer time village cricket is the delight of everyone.

   2.   Nearly every village has its own cricket field where the young men play and the old men watch.

      3.   In the village of Lintz in County Durham they have their own ground where they have played these last 70 years.

         4.   They tend it well.

---

[6]   *Miller* v. *Jackson*, [1977] 3 All ER 338 (CA), Lord Denning.

5. The wicket area is well rolled and mown.

5. The outfield is kept short.

4. It has a good clubhouse for the players and seats for the onlookers.

4. The village teams play there on Saturdays and Sundays.

5. They belong to a league, competing with the neighboring villages.

5. On other evenings after work they practice while the light lasts.

1. Yet now, after these 70 years, a judge of the High Court has ordered that they must not play there anymore.

2. He has issued an injunction to stop them.

3. He has done it at the instance of a newcomer who is no lover of cricket.

4. This newcomer has built, or had built for him a house on the edge of the cricket ground.

5. No doubt the open space was a selling point.

4. Now he complains that, when a batsman hits a six, the ball has been known to land in his garden or on or near his house.

5. His wife has got so upset about it that they always go out at weekends.

5.   They do not go into the garden when cricket is being played.

5.   They say that this is intolerable.

4.   So they asked the judge to stop the cricket being played.

3.   And the judge, much against his will, has felt that he must order the cricket to be stopped; with the consequences, I suppose, that the Lintz Cricket Club will disappear.

4.   The cricket ground will be turned to some other use.

5.   I expect for more houses or a factory.

4.   The young men will turn to other things instead of cricket.

4.   The whole village will be poorer.

3.   And all this because of a newcomer who has just bought a house there next to the cricket ground.

CHAPTER 12

FOURTH REVISION

SENTENCES

SENTENCE CHECKLIST

For your fourth revision, carefully review your sentences. Watch for five factors.

- First, make sure all your sentences are, in fact, sentences.

- Second, bring all the central elements of the sentence core together in one place.

- Third, check that the central action of the sentence is expressed in a verb and not a noun.

- Fourth, make sure that verb is in the active voice.

- Finally, check the length of your sentence; is it too long, incorporating more than one idea?

If you want to improve the quality of writing, this check is perhaps the most critical of all the revisions. I find that virtually every piece of legal writing I have reviewed for my students needs improvement in this area.

Therefore, I want you to specifically and consciously ask yourself these questions about each of your sentences. Stop on each one. Identify the subject, verb and, if required, object (Is it a sentence?). Are they right next to each other (Is the core together?). Is the central action of the sentence expressed in a verb?

Is that verb in the active voice? Does the sentence contain only one idea?

Certainly, as your skill grows, you will be able to write perfectly good sentence that doesn't follow all these rules. But for 99 out of 100 sentences, these are the rules that work.

Remember, I am not prescribing what is good writing. I'm trying to describe it to you and show you how to do it.

So, let's look at each item on the checklist in detail.

Is It A Sentence?

First, make sure all your sentences are, in fact, sentences. Remember that each sentence must have a *subject* and a *verb*. Usually, it will also have an *object.*

The subject of a sentence is a noun or pronoun and is the person, place or thing that the sentence talks about.

The verb is the action word of the sentence.

The object, if there is one, is again a noun or pronoun and is the person, place or thing that is the goal of the action.

The boy hit the ball.

In that sentence, *boy* is the subject, *hit* is the verb and *ball* is the object.

By making sure each sentence has at least a subject and a verb, you will avoid sentence fragments. A sentence fragment is a collection of words on the page that are punctuated like a sentence but which lack one of the essential elements of a sentence. Like this.

Some sentences, the shortest sentences, seem to break the first rule and lack a subject. They are just one word long. Stop. Go. Read. All three of those

sentences contain just a verb. However, each *does* have a subject, an implied "you" so they do follow the rule.

Is the Central Action in a Verb?

The verb is the *central action* around which the rest of the sentence is built. As we have seen, it is the most critical word in any sentence. Yet often, you will see sentences where this central action has been turned into a noun, a *thing* word. Sentences where the central action is expressed in a noun are flat and lifeless. Turn the central action back into a verb and you'll make the sentence much more readable.

Here's an example of a sentence where the central action is in a noun:

> We made a decision to have a discussion of the subject.

In this sentence there are actually two perfectly good verbs—*decide* and *discuss*—turned into the nouns *decision* and *discussion*. But turn them back into verbs and the sentence becomes more readable and, as a bonus, shorter.

> We decided to discuss the subject.

The way to spot verbs turned into nouns is to look for certain endings on words: _ion, and _ment are the two main ones. If you are working on a computer, you can use your word processor's ability to search for words to find those that end in _ion and _ment. Then you can check those words to make sure you're not needlessly turning a verb into a noun.

Is the Sentence in the Active Voice?

The next question you want to ask about each sentence is whether it is in the active voice.

In the active voice, the action is conveyed from a doer, the *subject* of the sentence, through the verb to a goal, the *object* of the sentence.

> The boy hit the ball.

In that sentence, the boy, the subject of the sentence, carries the action of hitting through to his goal, the ball, the object of the sentence.

There is another way to write that sentence that we call the passive voice:

> The ball was hit by the boy.

Notice that the object of the action, *ball*, has been turned into the grammatical subject of the sentence.

The passive voice has two hallmarks: it always includes a form of the verb *to be* attached to other verbs and it often includes the word *by*. Look at the example again. "The boy *was* hit *by* the ball."

You'll have to keep your eyes open for forms of *to be* on your own but you can a word processor's word search ability to hunt for *by*. When you spot the word *by*, check the sentence very carefully. If it's in the passive voice, see if you can convert it into the active voice.

ADVANTAGES OF THE ACTIVE VOICE

The best thing about the active voice is that it is clearer. In an active sentence, you know exactly who is doing what. Passive sentences are impersonal and lack vigor. They can lead to fuzziness, wordiness, awkwardness, and even grammatical error.

Let me give you a legal example. In a lease for a house you might find a sentence that reads,

> The pool shall be cleaned once a week.

Who is to do the cleaning? Is it the tenant or the landlord? Or is that sentence merely a statement of fact; the neighbor does it as a good deed every Saturday? In that passive sentence, it is never clear.

Certainly there are occasions where the passive voice is appropriate but they are rare. As a general rule, stick with the active.

Is the Core Together?

When all the elements in the sentence core—the subject, verb and object—are close to each other the sentence is easy to understand. They should be right next to each other. Here's an example of a poorly written sentence where the sentence core is spread all over:

> The boy [subject], after swinging mightily as no one in Pawtucket County had ever swung before, hit [verb], with such a force that it knocked off the cover, the ball [object].

Just listen to how it reads when all I do is put the core elements together and position the extraneous information before and after the core.

> After swinging mightily as no one in Pawtucket County had ever swung before, the boy hit the ball with such a force that it knocked off the cover.

A clumsy, hard to understand sentence becomes one that is clear and easy to understand.

Sentence Length

Finally, police your sentences for length. An average sentence length of 15-17 words is very readable. Let it climb much over 20 and you are getting into trouble. (The average length of sentences in this book is just under 15 words.)

One way to do that is to make sure each sentence contains only one idea. You can spot sentences with more than one idea because they contain more than one verb. Multiple verbs are not always bad. Many good sentences are compound or complex sentences but if you spot more than one verb in your sentence, look it over carefully and ask whether it is legitimately compound or complex or whether it just seems to wander on too long. (By the way, that last sentence is a perfect example of a compound/complex sentence; it contains six verbs, *are*, *spot*, *look*, *ask*, *is* and *seems*, yet works just fine.)

Earlier in the book, we looked at part of a statement of claim that contained one huge sentence. It read like this:

> The Plaintiff's claim against the Defendants, and each of them, is for general and special damages for loss and expense suffered and incurred by the Plaintiff arising out of paint particle overspray damage to the Plaintiff's vehicles and property located at or about 1991 Lougheed Highway, in the Municipality of Port Coquitlam, in the Province of British Columbia, which damage occurred on or about the 6th day of August, 1981, as a result of painting operations negligently carried on by the Defendants and or its servants/agents or employees which said negligence caused paint particles to escape and/or be wind-borne to the said premises of the Plaintiff causing extensive paint particle overspray damage to the Plaintiff's vehicles and property, and the Plaintiff claims for costs.

While compound and complex sentences have their places, this one certainly gets carried away. That single sentence is 127 words long. It encompasses no fewer than ten ideas.

1.   This claim is for general and special damages.

2.   It covers losses and expenses.

3.   It arises from spray paint damage to the plaintiff's property.

4.   The plaintiff's property was located at 1991 Lougheed Highway, Port Coquitlam, British Columbia.

5.   The damage occurred on August 6, 1981.

6.   It was the result of the defendant's painting operations.

7.   The defendant was negligent in its painting operation.

8.   The defendant's negligence allowed paint particles to blow over to the plaintiff's car lot.

9.   The paint particles landed on the plaintiff's vehicles and other property.

10.   The Plaintiff is also claiming its court costs.

Now, quite frankly, just breaking things up into those ten separate sentences would make a better statement of claim.

> This claim is for general and special damages. It covers losses and expenses. It arises from spray paint damage to the plaintiff's property. The plaintiff's property was located at 1991 Lougheed Highway, Port Coquitlam, British Columbia. The damage occurred on August 6, 1981. It was the result of the defendant's painting operations. The defendant was negligent in its painting operation. The defendant's negligence allowed paint particles to blow over to the plaintiff's car lot. The paint particles landed on the plaintiff's vehicles and other property. The Plaintiff is also claiming its court costs.

While that is a big improvement over the original, here's a better rewrite. Now that I've clarified the information in the original claim, I'm able to combine some of it again here but now it has some sense to it.

> On August 6, 1981, the defendant, Canadian Pacific Limited (CPL) was spray painting near 1991 Lougheed Highway, Port Coquitlam, British Columbia, the business location of the plaintiff, Kern Chevrolet Oldmobile Ltd. (Kern). CPL negligently allowed the wind to carry paint to Kern's premises where it splattered on Kern's property.

> As a result, Kern claims general and special damages and costs from the CPR.

That is a total of 63 words in three sentences. Average length is 21 words. The longest is 32 words, the others 17 and 14.

The first two sentences tell what happened. In those two sentences I show it is the defendant's actions at issue [item 6], make the allegation of negligence [item 7] and show the causal connection between the negligence and the damage [items 8 and 9]. I also deal with the date [item 5] and place [item 4].

Next, I say what the plaintiff is claiming [items 1 and 10 in the list of ideas in the original paragraph]. I've dropped the reference to "for loss and expenses" [item 2] because that is self evident. (If you don't think it is, add another sentence to my paragraph that says, "As a result, the plaintiff has had to spend $100,000 repainting the cars and has lost business worth $250,000." That makes it explicit. However, in my opinion, that is a matter to be proved at trial.)

I do not repeat the language of the original pleading about "defendant, its servants/agents or employees" because that is redundant. A person is always liable for the actions of his or her employees (the same as servants) and agents.

ONE BY ONE

If you only pay attention to one part of this book, this
is the chapter. If each of your sentences meets the
five criteria in this chapter, you will have gone a long
way toward improving your writing.

CHAPTER 13

FIFTH REVISION

DICTION

Diction is choosing just the right word and it is the subject of your fifth revision. Webster's Ninth New Collegiate Dictionary defines diction as "Choice of words especially with regard to correctness, clearness or effectiveness." If you want to writing to be as correct, clear and effective as possible, you must pay attention to the words you use.

Remember the example in chapter nine of a lawyer's letter offering to settle a wrongful dismissal claim for "Gross bi-monthly pay in the amount of $1,750.00 less withholding tax at 27% which amounts to a net payment of $1,220.00." We looked at it then because the lawyer had failed to check her mathematics on her truth and accuracy check.

Not only do the numbers in that sentence fail to add up, but the author has also misused the word *bi-monthly*. Bi-monthly means once every two months (bi = two). I doubt very much that the person in question made only $1,750 for two months work, particularly since this particular person was an executive. What the author of that letter probably meant was *semi-monthly* which means twice a month (semi = half). (Of course, semi-monthly is not the same as *bi-weekly* which means every two weeks.)

When you are checking your diction, you have to be sure you are using the right word correctly. There's one rule here: if you even think you have a hint that you might just possibly have an inkling of a shadow of a doubt about the meaning of a word, then **LOOK IT UP!**

The English language is extremely rich in vocabulary. Somewhere out there is the *one* word you want to exactly express the idea that's in your head. Don't give up until you find it. Mark Twain summed it up this way: "The difference between the right word and the almost right word is the difference between lightning and lightning bug."

Don't settle for a jar full of fireflies when you are searching for a bolt of inspiration.

APPROPRIATENESS

The first question to ask yourself when you are reviewing your diction is, "Have I used language that is appropriate for this audience, purpose and occasion?" If you are writing for someone else—drafting an affidavit, for example—are you using the language that person would use?

That also means are you using the language that the audience expects. For example, one of the people who read and provided me with comments on this book suggested quite strongly that, while it was appropriate to refer to American judges as "Justice Jones," that Canadian judges should called "Mr. Justice Jones." Reflecting my preference for the simpler, shorter version of almost anything—and perhaps my Yankee upbringing—I disagreed. But I appreciate the point of view and I spent a few moments considering just which form was appropriate.

SIMPLER IS BETTER

Keep the language as simple as possible, language which anyone can easily understand. It's easier to make simple language more sophisticated than it is to make gobbledy-gook clear.

So, whenever you have the choice between two words, a polysyllabic monster and a simple, one-syllable cretin, choose the cretin. Your writing is not a chance to brag about your expansive vocabulary. Stick to the simple, everyday words that everyone understands. If you fell you simply must use a big word, make absolutely certain that its meaning is plain from its context. DO NOT make your reader reach for the dictionary. You're not the *Building a Better Vocabulary* section of *Reader's Digest*.

Keep it simple.

No Presumptions

Never make any presumptions about your audience. Expressions that seem quite mundane to you can leave a client baffled. I recently got a call from a friend who is attempting to have an increase in child support enforced in another province. When her case had gone to court in British Columbia, her lawyer had been paid by the province's legal aid system. However, that system doesn't generally pay for a lawyer out of the province. Her lawyer sent he all the paperwork and wrote,

> I suggest that you now attend before the Legal Services Commission with these documents in hand and request that they appoint reciprocal counsel for you in Fort Francis. The only other alternative is for you to contact Fort Francis counsel directly and for you to retain them privately.

I'm sure that makes perfect sense to you but it certainly didn't to her. I told her he lawyer was saying, "You should take the paperwork to Legal Aid and ask if they'll pay for a lawyer for you in Fort Francis. If not, you'll have to hire one yourself."

People on the street don't speak of "retaining counsel." They "hire a lawyer." They don't know the difference between a barrister, a solicitor and an attorney-at-law—and don't particularly care. Don't presume you are speaking the same language. It's *your* job to translate from legalese to English, not your reader's.

AMBIGUITY AND VAGUENESS

When reviewing for diction, watch carefully for ambiguous words. An ambiguous word is one that can have more than one meaning. It is not the same as vagueness. Think of them this way. A word is like a fence around a piece of intellectual territory. It defines a group of ideas. An ambiguous word is really two fences around two acreages which may or may not be related. A vague word just surrounds a large area.

For example, the word *plane* is ambiguous. It can mean an *airplane,* a *flat surface,* a *carpentry tool* for smoothing boards, or a variety of sycamore *tree.* The meaning is only made clear by the context of the word.

The word *aircraft* on the other hand is vague. It includes not only airplanes but also helicopters, sailplanes, gyrocopters and manned balloons.

Vagueness is acceptable in some circumstances, ambiguity never. You may choose to cast the wide net of a vague word if you want to encompass all the different ideas included in that word. Often, in negotiations, you need an vague word that will enclose enough territory to get both parties inside the fence. For example, in a loan, the bank doesn't want to be nailed down to specific dates and times for what it must do but the borrower doesn't want the bank free of all obligation. They may decide to accept the intentionally vague sentence, "The bank shall act as a reasonable lender," and trust that they will never have to go to court to find out just what that is.

Ambiguity, on the other hand, is just inviting your reader to pick the wrong category and come to the wrong conclusion. If I say that I will sell you my plane for $100, it's a good deal for an airplane but not so good if I'm really offering the block plane my father used in his garage workshop.

ABSTRACTIONS VS. CONCRETENESS

Sometimes writers take vagueness too far and move into *abstraction.* Most of the time you want to be as *concrete* in your language as possible. As a writer, you are trying to take ideas from your mind and transfer them intact to your reader's mind. You do that with concrete language.

Here's an example. I'm going to talk about a woman in a red dress. I'll bet as soon as you read that sentence, you pictured a woman in your mind wearing a red dress. Was it a red satin dress with a mini skirt and no sleeves? That happens to be the particular red dress I had in mind but by speaking in generalities I failed to give you the complete picture . . . and you made up one of your own.

So, avoid expressions like *motor vehicle accident.* Talk about a *car accident* or a *truck accident* or a *motorcycle accident.* Those I can see. A motor vehicle accident? What is that? Better yet, tell me it was an accident involving a blue, 1965 Mustang convertible driven by a woman in a red satin dress with a miniskirt and no sleeves.

Science fiction writer Ray Bradbury summed it up well when he suggested that writers "Assault the senses." We are sensual beings. Use your reader's senses to transfer the thoughts from your mind to your reader's.

FOREIGN WORDS

Another common mistake many writers make is to include bits and pieces of foreign languages in their writing. That does not impress your reader. Quite frankly, they don't care that you may know Latin or French or even Albanian.

If you are writing in English, stick with English. If you are writing in French, stick with French. If you are writing in Russian, stick with Russian. Don't jump around.

Of course, every language adopts words from other languages. For instance, this evening I'm going to eat *crepes* on the *patio* before going to the *rodeo*. But before you use a word or expression, make sure it is legitimately part of the language.

In particular, avoid Latin and Law French terms. Many lawyers have argued with me that these are "terms of art." Perhaps a few, but *very* few.

For every one of these foreign expressions, there is a plain English equivalent. *Per annum* = yearly. *Inter alia* = among other things. *Bona fide* = good faith. *Supra* = above. *Infra* = below. *Ibid* = see note xx. *Ad infinitum* = forever. *Ad nauseum* = until you barf (see section on unnecessarily colloquial language below). *A piratis et latronibus capta dominum non mutant* = capture by pirates and robbers does not change title. (I expect you have never seen the last but I'll bet money there is at least one lawyer in North America who, within the last year, argued a case on the basis of the "well know legal principal that *A piratis et latronibus capta dominum non mutant.*)

Perhaps even more insidious than Latin words and phrases are Latin abbreviations. These require double translation. So, as of today, why not drop

e.g.= exempli gratia = for example

i.e. = id est = that is

q.v. = quod vide = which see

and their ilk.

COLLOQUIALISMS

Also, watch your use of overly colloquial language. I'm hardly a formal writer, yet just a few sentences back, I almost said that buying my carpentry plane for $100 was a *rip-off*. Certainly, *rip-off* is in common enough usage as I write this but who knows about a year from now or a decade from now. Also, it may be in use only in one segment of the population. As you can see, I found a perfectly acceptable substitute that can be understood by *all* my readers, not just those who are or who have teenagers.

UNNECESSARY FORMALITY

The opposite of being too darn casual is being overly formal—stuffy. You do not need to refer to yourself as "the writer." "I" or "me" will do just fine. So, it's not necessary to say

> Should inquires arise, please don't hesitate to contact the writer.

You could simply say

> If you have any questions, give me a call.

If, when giving an opinion on behalf of your firm, you wish to use the imperial "we," go ahead but be sure to distinguish between when you are speaking on behalf of your colleagues and when you are simply speaking for yourself. I'm sure that when you are making theater plans for you and your spouse you switch back and forth between "we" and "I"—"We'll be there at six. I'll wear my suit." Writing for the firm is no different.

Another overly formal use I often see is *above noted*, or *above captioned*. Most often, these refer to a citation at the beginning of a letter. You know the kind. The one that really tells you nothing.

```
RE:     Jones vs. Jones
        File No 12345-9
```

The best way around this particular problem is not to use that kind of citation or, if you do, to make it clear in your first sentence just what the heck you are talking about.

```
RE:      Jones vs. Jones
         File No 12345-9
```

Dear Mr. Smith,

I'm writing about the status of the divorce proceedings between your client, Mary Margaret Jones, and mine, Michael Joseph Jones.

Notice, I didn't have to say *above captioned* once.

FREIGHT TRAINS

Freight trains are those incredibly long lists or words that supposedly increase precision ("docks, piers, quays, anchorage, roadstead, roads, ports, or harbors"). Of course, the correct way to increase precision is to use the right word in the first place (waterfront).

Sometimes it takes a little work finding just the right word and occasionally you do need more than one word. But automatically dispatching a freight train will not solve your drafting problems.

LIST OF PROHIBITED WORDS AND EXPRESSIONS

Here's a list of words and expressions you might want to drop from your vocabulary. They are certainly not words that I would want to use.

After many of the words, you'll find suggested alternatives. It was interesting that, in going through this list and trying to suggest plain English alternatives, I had to look up well over half of them to be sure just what they meant. I like to think that my repeated trips to the dictionary reflect the obscurity of many of these words, not the meagerness of my vocabulary.

Old and Middle English Words

These are words you just won't hear on a street corner unless you get lucky and perfect that time machine you've been working on.

aforesaid (Most of the time, this is completely redundant: "the aforesaid motor vehicle." Presuming there is no other car involved, "the car" would do quite nicely. If there is another car, then "the Mustang" or "the Coupé de Ville.")

behoof (usually seen in conveyances, " . . . to his use and behoof." Since it means "use," it is redundant. Drop it.)

bounden (means *obligatory* as in "our bounden duty." It is also redundant. Drop it as well.)

foregoing (what you've already said which, since you've said it, doesn't need saying again.)

forswear ("renounce")

forthwith ("immediately")

henceforth ("from now on")

hereafter ("from now on")

hereby (usually redundant. Drop it. "I hereby renounce my claim" becomes "I renounce my claim.")

herein ("in this document")

hereinabove ("what I've already said")

hereinafter ("what I'm going to say")

hereof ("of this")

heretofore ("previously")

herewith ("along with this")

hitherto ("up to now")

let (as in *let and hindrance*)

moreover ("further," "besides," "likewise," "in addition")

nowise ("in no manner")

said (as an adjective: "the said dog." 99% of the time it is redundant. The other 1% of the time it can be replaced by "the.")

saith ("says")

same (as a noun: "giving same to his daughter." Use "it" or some other pronoun. Watch your pronoun antecedents; a pronoun usually substitutes for the closest appropriate noun.)

thence ("from that time", "from that place.")

thenceforth ("from then on")

thereabout ("nearby")

thereafter ("from then on")

thereat ("there")

therefor (as distinguished from therefore. Therefor means "for this" or "for that" as in "We return thanks therefor." Just say, "Thanks," or "We return thanks for it.")

therefrom ("from that" or "from it")

therein ("in")

thereof (usually redundant; "the house and the site thereof" can become "the house and its site.")

thereon ("on"; usually redundant)

thereout (ditto)

thereover (ditto)

therethrough (ditto)

thereto (ditto)

theretofore (ditto)

thereunder (ditto)

therewith (ditto)

to wit ("specifically" or "for example")

whence (us another term of place: "from which he came.")

whensoever ("whenever")

whereas (drop it unless you are using it for "on the contrary": "I like dogs whereas my friend likes cats." For the recitals of a contract, just state the facts in single sentences. The use of "whereas" to begin contracts leads to a futile attempt to construct a single sentence 4,000 words long.)

whereat ("at what" or "at which")

whereby ("by which")

wherefore ("why")

wherein ("in what" or "in which")

whereof ("of what" or "of which")

whereon ("on what" or "on which")

whereupon ("after which")

whilst ("while")

witness (testimony "in witness of." Not needed. Drop it.)

witnesseth

Freight Trains

Some of these sets of coupled synonyms had historical legitimacy (which is often no longer legitimate.) Since our law developed as a merger of Norman law and Anglo-Saxon law, in Angevin England you often had to use both a Saxon and French word to make sure you had covered the bases. Of course, Henry II has been dead for a few years . . . .

As a very broad rule, you can use one of these terms and it handles the other just fine. Before you use both, think about just what you are tying to say and whether you really need both.

acknowledge and confess

act and deed

annul and set aside

authorize and empower

conjecture and surmise

covenant and agree (covenant and contract merged a long, long time ago. "Agree" will do quite nicely.)

cover, embrace and include ("include")

deem and consider

due and payable

each and all

each and every

entirely and completely

final and conclusive

fit and proper

fit and suitable

for and during

for and in consideration of

force and effect

fraud and deceit

free and unfettered

from and after

give and grant

give, devise and bequeath (The difference between a devise and a bequest was long ago abolished in most jurisdictions by a *Wills Act* or its equivalent. This really says "give, give and give." One is sufficient.)

goods and chattels

have and hold

heed and care

hold and keep

hold, perform, observe, fulfill and keep

in lieu, in place, instead and in substitution of

in my stead and place

in truth and in fact

just and reasonable

keep and maintain

last will and testament (A will and a testament are now the same in most common law jurisdictions.)

let or hindrance

lot, tract, or parcel of land

made and provided

made, ordained, constituted and appointed

maintenance and upkeep

meet and just

mind and memory

modified and changed

null and void ("void")

null, void and of no legal force or effect ("void")

of and concerning

ordered, adjudged and decreed

over, above and in addition to

pardon and forgive

part and parcel

peace and quiet

remise, release and quitclaim

rest, residue and remainder ("rest")

revoked, annulled and held for nought

save and except

seised and possessed

shun and avoid

situate, lying and being in

stand remain and be

truth and veracity

void and of no effect
("void")

void and of non
effect ("void")

void and of no force
("void")

will and testament

void and of no
value ("void")

Legal Formality

These are phrases and word that are seen nowhere
but in legal documents. They qualify as the height of
legalese. Most of them can just be dropped. If you
feel that something must be said, then figure out what
these say and say it plainly. Justice William A.
Bablitch of the Wisconsin Supreme Court calls such
language "flamboyance from another age. Spare the
reader—this is the 90's." [1]

are held and firmly bound

be it remembered

by virtue of the authority vested in me

came on for hearing

deposes and says

for such other and further relief as this Court may
deem meet and just (The Rules of Court in many
jurisdictions explicitly say that the court can grant
any relief that it is within it's power to grant
whether or not it is requested. So, you don't need
this kind of blanket request.)

from the beginning of the world to the present
("always")

further affiant saith not (altogether unnecessary)

---

[1]   William A Bablitch, *Writing to Win*, The Compleat Lawyer,
       Winter 1988.

further deponent saith not (ditto)

in witness whereof I have hereunto set my hand and caused the seal of . . . to be affixed (The execution of a document need not be particularly noted as long as it is clear that the parties knew they were signing something important—and that is always a triable question of fact.)

in witness whereof the parties hereto have hereunto executed this agreement the day and year first above written (ditto)

Know All Men By These Presents

make oath and saith ("swears" or "says under penalty of perjury")

Plaintiff complains of defendant and for cause of action alleges

respectfully submit

set down for hearing

strangers to the blood

the undersigned

time is of the essence (I don't think you could still win a case based on a simple statement that "Time is of the essence," particularly if it involved a consumer contract. Why not include a clause that explains this. "The parties agree that the deadlines in this contract will be strictly enforced. Failure to meet a deadline will give the other party the right to rescind the contract.")

Wherefore, defendant prays that plaintiff takes nothing

without merit

Witnesseth

CHAPTER 14

SIXTH REVISION

GRAMMAR, SPELLING AND PUNCTUATION

You're almost done. There's one last revision you want to make on your document. That's a final proofread for grammar, spelling and punctuation.

There is *nothing* that can replace a careful, slow proofread. There's no way to avoid it. While there are computer programs that will help check your spelling, grammar and punctuation, I guarantee that you can pass your document through every one and it will still have mistakes in it. So, look on these programs as assistants only.

Of course, you undoubtedly spotted many of the errors during previous revisions and probably marked them. Now is the time to go back and fix them. Then you still have to read through your document again, word by word, looking for more errors.

STYLE GUIDES

Grammar, punctuation and spelling fall into the general category of usage or style. As with diction, there's one unbreakable rule here: if you even think you have a hint that you might just possibly have an inkling of a shadow of a doubt about word usage, punctuation or spelling, then LOOK IT UP! (Is this starting to sound familiar?)

There are literally dozens of reference works that can help you with grammar and usage questions. They're often called style manuals. Style manuals answer those pesky questions about word usage (when to use less and when to use fewer, the difference between flout and flaunt) as well as punctuation issues (Just when do you use a semicolon?) and even the spelling of tough words.

If you don't have a style guide, get one.

A Personal List of Style Guides

Here's a list of style guides. It is not meant to be the definitive list of books on style issues. It quite wantonly reflects the ones that I like and find myself using day in and day out.

- *English Simplified*, Blanche Ellsworth and John A. Higgins, Longman, 2009.

- *Modern English Usage,* H.W. Fowler, revised by Sir Earnest Gowers, Oxford University Press, first edition 1926 with frequent reissues.

- *The Chicago Manual of Style,* 13th ed., University of Chicago Press, 1982.

- *The Associated Press Stylebook*, Basic Books, New York, updated annually.

- *The Canadian Press Stylebook: A Guide for Writers and Editors*, The Canadian Press, Toronto, first printed in 1940. Updated every few years.

- *The Canadian Style: A Guide to Writing and Editing*, Dundrum Press, 1997. The Canadian government's style manual.

- *The New York Times Manual of Style and Usage*, Times Books, 2002.

Also, the *Los Angeles Times* and many other major newspapers make their internal style guides available to the public for a reasonable price.

GRAMMAR AND PUNCTUATION

I'm not going to belabor my point that there's only one way to learn grammar and punctuation and that is through practice, careful proofing and looking up every questionable usage.

But let me give you one tip about punctuation that is often overlooked. The proper way to punctuate is by the paragraph and not by the sentence. This follows from paragraphs being the basic unit of thought in English. So, you have to punctuate your paragraph as a unit.

Here's an example from Jacob Bronowski's book, *The Common Sense of Science*: [1]

> This brings me to the third failing of eighteenth century science, which I find most interesting. A science with orders its thought too early is stifled. For example, the ideas of the Epicureans about atoms two thousand years ago were quite reasonable; but they did only harm to a physics which could not measure temperature and pressure and learn the simpler laws that relate them. Or again, the hope of the medieval alchemists that the elements might be changed was not as fanciful as we once thought. But it was merely damaging to a chemistry which did not yet understand the composition of water and common salt.

Can you spot what is wrong with the punctuation in that paragraph? Few people can, but if we dissect it with Christensen's paragraph analysis system, it starts to become obvious.

1. This brings me to the third failing of eighteenth century science, which I find most interesting.

---

[1] Jacob Bronowski, *The Common Sense of Science*, Harvard University Press, 1952.

2. A science with orders its thought too early is stifled.

3. For example, the ideas of the Epicureans about atoms two thousand years ago were quite reasonable;
but
they did only harm to a physics which could not measure temperature and pressure and learn the simpler laws that relate them.

3. Or again, the hope of the medieval alchemists that the elements might be changed was not as fanciful as we once thought.

4. But it was merely damaging to a chemistry which did not yet understand the composition of water and common salt.

Look at the two sentences at level 3. Both are examples and both are subject to exceptions introduced by "but." However, in the first case, Bronowski used a semicolon as a conjunction between two independent clauses. In the second case, he punctuated with a period and started a new sentence.

Now don't get me wrong. Either punctuation *on its own* is fine. However, they cannot coexist in the same paragraph. One has to change to match the other. He has constructed two *parallel* sentences and parallel structures require parallel punctuation.

Bronowski's mistake is a perfect example of a really subtle error. In the eleven years I have been using this paragraph as an example in my workshops, only two students have been able to spot the error and both had been writing professionals of some kind before they became lawyers.

But you have to pursue that kind of excellence in writing, right down to the sometimes ridiculous details, if you want to be a good writer.

SPELLING

Like grammar and punctuation, learning to spell correctly involves a lot of time looking things up. I have three dictionaries in my office, the closest about a foot and a half away as I write. Keep your dictionary with you as you write. If you are at all like me, if you have to walk across the room to get the dictionary, you are more likely to say, "Oh, I think that's OK." And you know the way life works: if you think it's OK, it's not.

The same rule applies to spelling as to other questions of usage and style: **LOOK IT UP!** Don't think. Just look things up. If you even think of questioning a spelling, pull down the dictionary.

Remember, also, that we all have "blind spots" when it comes to spelling. There are a couple of dozen words that I can't spell correctly no matter how hard I try. It's primarily a matter of confidence; I've misspelled them so many times in the past that even when I get them right I'm not sure of myself, so I look them up again.

There is a set of spelling rules you should know at the end of the book. They deal with most of the everyday spelling quandaries you might run into.

A DIGRESSION ON LAYOUT AND DESIGN

This is not a book on graphic design, but before you send any piece of writing out of your office, make sure that it is attractive and the kind of document someone will want to read.

Margins

In particular, do you have margins at least an inch wide. An inch and a half would be even better. Too often I see letters and memos that must come from law firms that are on the brink of financial collapse. That's the only rational explanation for the stinginess they're showing with paper, cramming text from the top to the bottom and side to side. I've seen law firms that have actually typed right over part of their letterhead at the bottom of the page!

Come on. Paper is cheap. Your client is paying you $100 an hour or more. Don't begrudge her three cents worth of paper.

Headings

Most law firms today are using computers to generate most of their documents. Are you using the full potential of your printer and word processing software?

Getting the most out of a word processor and printer requires expertise. That means you're going to have to hire someone to come in and fine tune them. But, in addition to producing better looking documents, you can actually save money on printing bills. Take a look at how much you spend just printing letterhead each year. For someone who knows what he or she is doing, it's not difficult to reproduce almost any letterhead on a laser printer. In the past year, I've helped several firms say good-bye to letterhead printing bills forever. Now, at the same time as it produces the letter, their laser printer prints their letterhead. When the list of partners changes, it's a simple task to adjust the letterhead without having to turn 5,000 sheets of old letterhead into scratch paper.

PART V

PLAIN SPEAKING

The overriding objective is simplicity and
conciseness. The issues should be as few as
possible and stated as simply as possible.

Justice William A. Bablitch
Supreme Court of Wisconsin

CHAPTER 15

THE CASE FOR PLAIN ENGLISH

WHY WRITE PLAINLY?

I expect that by now you've noticed my bias in favor of plain English writing. I unabashedly promote plain English writing in this book and in my workshops. I believe, both as a writer and a lawyer, that it is *always* better to express yourself simply, clearly and simply in the language in which you are working.

We looked at a few reasons legal writing is as poor as it is early in the book: habit, bad examples and history. Here are a few more: the mistaken idea that legal writing is more *precise*, that it is *well-settled* and that legal ideas are just *too complex* to be stated simply.

Precision

Is convoluted legal writing more precise? I doubt it. For centuries lawyers have tried to make their writing more precise and, as you probably have noticed, we're not a whole lot closer to true precision than when the first proto-lawyers were arguing in Latin before Henry II.

The precision in writing comes, if anywhere, in simple language. "The plaintiff is John Doe, a carpenter. The defendant is ABC Corp., a pharmaceutical company. In 1982, Mr. Doe purchased a drug manufactured by ABC Corp. When he took the drug, it crippled him."

English—even the plainest English—is a remarkably complex language. The roots of the language have come from both the Germanic and Romance traditions. In addition, we've adopted thousands of words from other languages. *Somewhere* in the language is the *one* word you need for the idea you are trying to express. Your job is to find that one word.

Sometimes that right word *is* a true magic word. There are some in the law. But even magic words can be used simply. "Mr. Jones put the money in trust for his children," not "Mr. Jones, by deed executed under seal, settled the monies upon his two lawful offspring, in trust for their sole benefit and use."

Well Settled

The second argument is that the language of the law is "tried and true," that the old legal language has been to court and its meaning clarified. One lawyer put it this way: [1]

> Legalese evolved because the meaning of a word or phrase frequently had gone to court . . . . This process has meant that legal language gradually has become precise and relatively certain . . . . Thus, one can depend upon what the particular words mean (or certainly what they do not mean) because a court has ruled, and probably would rule in the future, that they mean just that.

Notice by the way, that even the defenders of legal vocabulary don't defend the circumlocutious construction, the word lists, the verbs made into nouns, passive voice, negatives, split verbs and other grammatical absurdities.

Certainly, if you truly believe that a certain phrasing is truly magic, then use it. But don't kid yourself that even if a word has been litigated, its meaning is settled. Each time a word goes back into court, its legal meaning moves just as its everyday meaning has

---

[1] William C. Prather, "In Defence of the People's Use of Three Syllable Words," 39 Ala. Lawyer 394, 395 (1978).

moved. Language is not static. It changes, develops, grows.

Professor Robert Benson phrases the question about whether a meaning is well-settled—and thus a true magic word—this way: [2]

> Does the term have an uncontroversial core meaning that could not be conveyed succinctly in any other way? If so, it is a true term of art.

That said, Benson estimates that the true terms of art are no more than a hundred including *plaintiff* and *defendant, estoppel, ex parte, res judicata, hearsay* and *injunction.*

He specifically excludes "*heir, seisin, premises, and/or, may, shall . . . aforesaid, said* (instead of *the*), *such* (instead of *that*), *same* (as a pronoun), *hereinafter, therein, thereto, thereof, whereas, whereby, wherein* or *witnesseth . . . cease and desist, free and clear, null and void, acknowledge and confess, by and through, each and every, force and effect, from and after, made and entered into* or *true and correct.*" [3]

You've already seen the list of words I would exclude (in Chapter 13).

Remember that the first rule of interpretation is to look at the *plain meaning* of the words. That means that the first place a lawyer or judge must turn when

---

[2]   Robert W. Benson, "Plain English Comes to Court," Litigation, Volume 13, Number 1, Fall 1986, page 24. This article is a short summary of empirical research Benson has done showing that plain English documents are quite simply more convincing and more effective legal documents. The full details of his research are in "Legalese v. Plain English: An Empirical Study of Persuasion and Credibility in Appellate Brief Writing," 20 Loyola of Los Angeles Law Review 301, January 1987 and in "The End of Legalese: The Game is Over," XIII Review of Law and Social Change 519.

[3]   Robert W. Benson, "Plain English Comes to Court," Litigation, Volume 13, Number 1, Fall 1986, page 24.

trying to understand a particular passage is to a *conventional* dictionary, not a legal dictionary.

Also, remember that if a judge or group of judges really decides that you are going to lose, they are going to work their way around any language you can create. There's no such thing as watertight drafting.

Too Complex

The next argument against simple language in legal writing is that the functions of legal documents are too complex, the ideas they express too sophisticated for simplicity.

To which I say, "bunkum." Nobel Prize winner John Kenneth Galbraith says the same thing with a bit more sophistication. [4]

> There are no important propositions that cannot be stated in plain language . . . The writer who seeks to be intelligible needs to be right; he must be challenged if his argument leads to an erroneous conclusion and especially if it leads to the wrong action. But he can safely dismiss the charge that he has made the subject too easy. The truth is not difficult.

"PERFORMATIVES" VS. "REAL DOCUMENTS"

Loyola's Benson divides legal documents into two categories, *performatives* — documents that *do* something like start a lawsuit or file a motion — and *real documents* which actually *say* something.

Some American jurisdictions are doing away with performatives and replacing them with forms where all you do is check off the appropriate box. No one ever

---

[4]   John Kenneth Galbraith, "Writing, Typing and Economics," The Atlantic Monthly, March 1978.

really looked at the other documents anyway. The form was what mattered.

But the real documents, facta and other arguments that need to make a real impact, actually work better when they are written clearly and plainly.

In an article on writing appellate briefs, Justice William Bablitch of the Wisconsin Supreme Court says it pretty clearly himself.

> Looking for a model? Carefully read your newspaper. Watch how a good reporter takes you through a story: short, simple sentences, paragraphs; flow. Compare that with your writing. [5]

Simplicity in Practice

The Santa Monica, California, firm of Fadem, Berger and Norton, had an editor on their staff who read every piece of paper that went out the door. Consequently, they turned out readable, persuasive documents that won cases. Here are some samples from a brief the firm prepared for a successful California Supreme Court case. The brief is in response to a friend-of-the-court (not *amicus curiae*) brief from San Diego and Orange Counties. [6]

> This is an airport noise case. From the cases cited in the San Diego/Orange brief, one would conclude that there has never been another decision dealing with airport noise liability. Some of the omitted cases deal directly with the question of "federal pre-emption" and its impact on airport operator liability. If San Diego and Orange were "friends" of this Court, wouldn't they at least

---

[5]   William A Bablitch, *Writing to Win*, The Compleat Lawyer, Winter 1988.

[6]   Quoted in Robert W. Benson, "Plain English Comes to Court," Litigation, Volume 13, Number 1, Fall 1986, page 25.

---

mention these cases to give the Court the
proper background . . . ?

Power and responsibility: That's what it's all
about. Having grudgingly conceded the
existence of their *own* power, San Diego and
Orange insist that *no one may compel* them to
exercise that power.

But no one has sought to.

No injunctive relief is sought.

If, as the San Diego/Orange brief urges,
airport operators should be free to exercise
their power as they see fit, well and good.

But power carries its concomitant
responsibility. It is the possession of power
by airport operators that renders them liable
for injuries inflicted on their neighbors.
Misuse it or fail to use it to protect, and
liability follows for the consequent damage.

And that simple concept is at the heart of this
case. If an airport operator chooses to use its
power tortiously, it ought to bear the
consequences. It is sheer brass to claim the
absolute right to act, and the absolute
immunity from the consequences.

Partner Jerrold Fadem explained that it paid to have
an editor. "It is not an uncommon experience for us to
appear for motions, have the judge indicate a
predisposition to the view expressed by our papers, sit
through a colloquy between judge and adversary
lawyer, and depart without having said anything but
our name for the record and thank you at the end."[7]

---

[7]   Jerrold Fadem, "Legalese as Legal Does: Lawyers Clean Up
Their Act," Prosecutor's Brief 14 (Jan-Feb 1979).

A Canadian Perspective

Since I live and often teach in Canada, I often hear, "Ah, but those are Americans. Our Canadian judges are much more conservative. They'd never put up with language like that."

Well, let me tell you what at least one of those conservative Canadian judges — Justice M.R. Taylor of the British Columbia Supreme court — has to say about the use of language.[8]

> I have drawn an analogy with the art of the potter. Like lawyers, the potter must shape his material into things of practical use, but in such a way as will make them aesthetically attractive to the user. When we pare off an unnecessary sentence, smooth out an awkward phrase, reposition an ill placed verb, or throw away the whole mess and start again, we do as the potter does when he fashions his clay [and] finds a hole in his emerging jar or that his jug will not stand on its bottom, or that his Grecian urn has lost all hope of achieving its intended Attic beauty.
>
> After 35 years at the writer's wheel, I confess that I have learned very little indeed of the art which I am trying to describe.
>
> After 15 years in the newspaper business, there was only one piece of guidance I could remember. It was that of an old news editor who used to say that every story is an answer to the same question: "What happened?" After 15 years as a practicing lawyer, the only helpful advice I could recall receiving was

---

[8] Justice M.R. Taylor, Supreme Court of British Columbia, "Effective Legal Writing: The Lawyer's Role As Technician and Artist In The Written Word", The Advocate, Volume 40, November 1982.

that of a particularly wise colleague who said, "There is only one way to begin. You say, 'It's just this simple.'"

Four years on the bench have added nothing. When dealing with facts, I still try to answer the question: "What happened?" When handling the law, I try to find a way of saying, "It's just this simple."

. . .

I have said that the written word is our raw material. It is a raw material that comes to us without charge. We are as much free miners in the rich vein of the English language as in the wealth of the Common Law. Perhaps it might have been better if it were not so, if we were assessed a royalty for every word—better every syllable—that we took from the English dictionary. That might make us more careful in our writing habits, better choosers and users of the written word. But we ought not, in my view, to need that incentive. The profit which we as lawyers stand to gain from better use of written language seems to me quite obvious.

THE REAL REASONS

In addition to those well-worn arguments, a few other, more subtle elements seem to discourage plain legal writing. Please forgive me if I express them plainly. They are greed, fear and self-deception.

Greed

Another name for greed is "professional protection." Some lawyers fear that if their clients really understood what was going on, they would feel they don't need a lawyer anymore.

Economist John Kenneth Galbraith put it this way:[9]

> Complexity and obscurity have professional
> value — they are the academic equivalents of
> apprenticeship rules in the building trades.
> They exclude the outsiders, keep down the
> competition, preserve the image of a
> privileged or priestly class. The man who
> makes things clear is a scab. He is criticized
> less for his clarity than for his treachery.

Harvard's Steven Stark put it even more clearly.[10]

> Lawyers write badly because doing so
> promotes their economic interest.

Frankly, I don't think it's true that clients would desert lawyers if they understood what was going on. In fact, if they knew just what they were getting for their money, clients might be more comfortable with their lawyers and actually use more legal services.

The law *is* confusing, complicated and full of potential potholes. It takes an expert to find your way around. Lawyers know that perhaps better than anyone. It is rare you see a lawyer who handles his or her own legal affairs, especially as soon as he or she moves out of his or her personal area of expertise. Trust lawyers don't handle their own divorces and family lawyers don't draft merger contracts. In fact, few family lawyers do their own divorces.

So, even if lawyers let clients know exactly what is going on, believe me, they'll still need us.

---

[9]   John Kenneth Galbraith, "Writing, Typing and Economics," The Atlantic Monthly, March 1978.

[10]   Steven Stark, "Why Lawyers Can't Write," Bar Leader, Volume 10, Number 6, May-June 1985, pg 15.

Fear

My students, particularly the younger ones, often worry that if they simply say what they mean, they will be caught up in a web of convoluted interpretation rules. They are afraid of what they don't know, the obscure statute, the unknown magic words, the potential malpractice suits. They fear that if they leave out something — anything — they've seen in other similar documents, they'll make a mistake. As a result, they begin to uncritically imitate the poor writing they have seen.

But, again, the first rule of interpretation is that a court must look at the *plain meaning of the words.* Only when the words are not clear do you even have to worry about the other issues of interpretation. Make yourself clear in plain English using words as they are defined in a standard dictionary and you are on solid ground.

Self-Deception

Lawyers are perhaps the world's most respected con artists. By definition, half of the cases you take to court are going to be losers. Sometimes, the best thing you can do for your client is to confuse the hell out of the court and the opposition.

As Harvard's Steven Stark says,[11]

> Lawyers recognize their role as deceivers and understand that language is the means by which they work their magic. And, after a while, they lose their faith in the honesty of words.
>
> . . .

---

[11] Steven Stark, "Why Lawyers Can't Write," Bar Leader, Volume 10, Number 6, May-June 1985, pg 17.

To write as a lawyer is to choose a perspective that can cheapen language and force us to relate to a narrow world of rules, not people. In a sense, part of the purpose of legal training is to enable lawyers to think and write about cases . . . in just that way.

But perhaps lawyers lose more than they gain by acquiring the gift of legal vision. If so, complaints about legal writing are not really laments about craftsmanship; they are cries that lawyers can no longer hear.

If that is true, then *we* are the losers.

THE REAL REASON TO WRITE WELL

But I'm still avoiding the question. I'm telling you why the excuses for not writing well are not valid. That still doesn't tell you why you *should* write well. I think there are two reasons.

First, if you are like me, you like to do what you do as best you can. If you were satisfied with your writing, you wouldn't have read this book. So, getting better as what you do is probably satisfaction enough for most of us.

But you may need a reason for the managing partner as well. It's this: writing well will make you a better lawyer. You'll be more convincing and win more cases in court. Your drafting will be tighter (and shorter) and actually more litigation proof. You'll make your clients happier, do a better job and — as a side benefit — make more money.

That's a reason that would appeal to the heart of a Douglas Brackman.

PUTTING IT INTO ACTION

Writing well when all around you are producing trash takes strength of character. Others will want you to write as poorly as they do because they are embarrassed by how well you do it — and how poorly they do. They'll throw up all the objections we've seen in this book and a lot more I haven't thought of. "It's unprofessional," "It's secretarial," "It doesn't sound like a lawyer," and many more.

You just keep doing what you know how to do: write well, from your gut. Don't let you head get in the way too early on and you'll do just fine.

If you have to time, I'd like to hear about your experiences and how what you've learned in this book has affected your work. Please write me in care of the publisher. Who knows, you may end up as one of the quotes in the next edition.

Good luck. And thanks for sticking with me to the end.

PART VI

EXAMPLES

NOTES ON THE EXAMPLES

In this section, I have included several examples of typical legal documents. First come a few letters to clients and other lawyers, then a factum, a contract and an opinion letter.

These samples (and the others in this section) come (with permission) from the files of a major law firm which will remain nameless to save them embarrassment.

I've introduced each document with some general comments followed by the document itself and, in several cases, rewrites. I've included comments on specific aspects of each document in footnotes. Occasionally, originals are marked with strike-through and bold text where I have edited them. Text to be deleted is ~~struck through~~. Text to be added is **bold**.

LETTERS

LETTER #1 -
FAMILY MATTERS

This letter is a typical example of a letter to a non-lawyer. Generally, the language is much too sophisticated for this audience. Language that seems everyday to us is not easy to understand for our clients. Remember my story about my friend who called to ask what "retain counsel" meant. I told her it meant "hire a lawyer." That's the kind of language you have to use in letters to clients.

Bright, Red and Scooter

Barristers and Solicitors

123 Granville St.
Toronto, Ontario M2T 2P3
(416) 555-1111

December 5, 1985

WITHOUT PREJUDICE

Mr. Rufus Hurricane
33 Holiday Trail
Unit 1
Sarnia, ONT

Dear Sir:

RE: Hurricane v. Hurricane

Further to our recent telephone conversation, I confirm you have advised me that you are now acting for yourself in this matter and do not intend to retain another solicitor.[1]

I enclose herein[2] draft Minutes of Settlement[3] for you to look at. They

---

[1]   Any letter that starts out "Further to . . . " is one where you haven't bothered to think about what you are really doing. You're falling back on bad habits. Don't be afraid to be friendly. It is *not* the opposite of businesslike.

>   Thanks for your time on the telephone last Tuesday. During our conversation you told me that you were now acting for yourself in this divorce and that you did not intend to hire another lawyer.

[2]   No one but a lawyer would ever intentionally use the word "herein." Why not say: "I have enclosed draft Minutes of Settlement for you to review."

basically are in accordance with[4] my letter to Mr. Cook of November 11, 1985.

Under these minutes of Settlement, you would immediately sign a deed to your condominium to you and Mrs. Hurricane as joint tenants.[5] This means that if one of you dies, the other automatically owns the whole thing.[6] This protects you for the next few years in that if Mrs. Hurricane dies, you would get the whole condominium back and be able to continue to run your business, and it also protects Mrs. Hurricane in that she would get something if you die, since you have now changed your life insurance.[7]

---

[3]   And while we're on the subject, just what are "Minutes of Settlement" in plain language?

[4]   They basically are the same as . . . .

[5]   This language would be very confusing to a lay person. They would speak of "signing over the condominium into the names of you and your wife as 'joint-tenants.'" (Note that the period *always* goes inside the quotation marks.)

[6]   Good explanation.

[7]   Although all the required information is in this paragraph, it is obscured by the writing. For instance, the last sentence is 53 words long. Try to say it in one breath and you'll be gasping. It contains two ideas and breaks nicely in two. Here's how I would rewrite.

> Under this agreement, you would immediately sign the papers necessary to transfer the title of your condominium into the names of you and your wife as joint tenants. This means that if one of you dies, the other automatically has sole title to the condo. This protects both of you. If Mrs. Hurricane died in the next few years, you would have clear title to the condominium and be able to continue your business. If you died, she would have something to replace the life insurance you have changed.

The rewrite has five sentences (average length 18.4 words) while the original had only three sentences (average length 29.9). The shorter sentences are easier for a reader to digest.

I have included a payment by you[8] to Mrs. Hurricane of $11,400.00 for her interest in the boat, the car and the contents of the apartment left with you. We[9] arrived at that figure as follows:

1. Value of Boat:$ 20,000.00

2. Value of Car: 2,800.00

3. Value of contents remaining
   in apartment   6,000.00

TOTAL: $ 28,800.00

One half of that total is $14,400.00. From that we have deducted $3,000.00 as Mrs. Hurricane's share of the bank loan. You may recall we[10] earlier determined that your bank loan was about $10,000 and that about $4,000.00 of that was used for the business float. There therefore remained[11] $3,000.00 as Mrs. hurricane's one-half share of the[12] loan which was for family purposes.

Mrs. Hurricane has agreed not to force the sale of the condominium until you turn sixty-five, [13] but, if you do not pay her the amount owing to her for her share of the

---

[8]   "I have included a payment" sounds like the author is sending the money. Adding "by you" further confuses the reader. What the author means to say is, "The settlement includes your payment to Mrs. Hurricane . . . ."

[9]   Which "we"? The author and the reader? The author and Mrs. Hurricane? This is a perfect example of an ambiguous word: it can have one of several meanings. Admittedly, the reader, knowing more about the case, would probably know, but what about a new lawyer taking over the file? Would he or she have any idea?

[10]   Same question about the "we".

[11]   Replace "There therefore remained" with "That left."

[12]   Add "part of the" so this reads "That left $3,000 as Mrs. Hurricane's one-half share of the part of the loan which was for family purposes."

[13]   Start a new sentence here.

boat, car, etc. by July 31, 1986, she will
be able to proceed with a sale of the
condominium.[14] the July, 1986 date was
chosen in order to give you time to effect
the sale or refinancing of the boat.[15]

As you know, Mrs. Hurricane is very
concerned about the regularity of the
support payments as she needs the money to
pay rent. I have therefore included a
clause that you provide her with post-dated
cheques each year and that these cheques
will be negotiable on the 16th of the month
in order to allow you to receive the rent
payment which I understand are the 15th of
the month.[16] The support payments will stop
if Mrs. Hurricane lives with another man, or
remarries, and they will be binding upon

---

[14]   Replace "She will be able to proceed with a sale of the
condominium" with "She may sell the condominium."

[15]   Replace "to effect the sale or refinancing of the boat" with "to
sell or refinance the boat." This is a good (or bad) example of
turning verbs (*to sell*, *to refinance*) into nouns (*sale,
refinancing*). The result is you need to add a verb (*to effect*) in
order to have a sentence. Why not just use the verbs you
started with.

The rewritten paragraph incorporating all the suggestions in
the last few notes would read:

Mrs. Hurricane has agreed not to force the sale of the
condominium until you turn sixty-five. However, if
you do not pay her the amount owing to her for her
share of the boat, car, etc. by July 31, 1986, she may
sell the condominium. The July, 1986, date was
chosen to give you time to sell or refinance the boat.

[16]   This sentence is too long. Split it in two. "I have therefore
included a clause that you provide her with post-dated
cheques. These cheques will be negotiable on the 16th of the
month . . . ."

Also, start a new paragraph here. The first half of this
paragraph as it is now talks about her concern for the support
payments. The second half talks about what happens if he
stops paying. Try to build a Christensen analysis of the
paragraph (see Chapter 11) as it currently stands and you'll
see why it has to be split.

your estate as a first charge against it [17] if you die. The amount of the support payments is variable by either of you [18] if your circumstances change.

I urge you to review this document with a solicitor [19] and to have him or her contact me if there are any questions. Please let me know immediately if you are prepared to sign it and if so, I can arrange to meet with you to sign the original. I will also need the deed to your condominium property in order to draw up a new deed transferring the property into both or your names.

I look forward to hearing from you as soon as possible.

Yours very truly,

BONNIE A. SCOOTER

---

[17]   Explain what this means.

[18]   Passive. "Either of you may apply to vary the payments . . . ." How?

[19]   Regular people talk of "lawyers," not "attorneys," "barristers" or "solicitors." "Barrister" and "solicitor" are particularly problematic. Most people have no idea whatsoever what a "barrister" is, and they believe a solicitor is someone who sells things door-to-door. That's why they have a sign on their door saying "No Solicitors."

LETTER #2 -
I LOVED YOU AND IT'S
GOING TO COST YOU

Generally, this letter isn't bad. Things I like about it:

- The author has paid attention to his audience. This is a "cover your behind" letter so that when the client sues the lawyer for not following his instructions, the lawyer has this on file outlining the instructions in writing. Therefore, it has two audiences: the client (to make sure the lawyer has the instructions right) and another lawyer who is suing the first some time in the future. The client wants to know that his lawyer is going to do what he said he would so. The future lawyer wants to find out where the first one screwed up. Generally, this letter deals with both well.

- It is not overly formal (until the end).

- It does not use the overly formal royal "we" so often seen in law firm letters. Nor does it indulge in the obnoxious habit of the author referring to herself as "the writer."

Scarlet, Rose and Indigo

Lawyers   100 - 100 Some Street
                                               Toronto, Ontario M5T 3T3
                                               Canada
                                               (416) 555-5555

March 10, 1986

Mr. Rufus Hurricane
33 Holiday Trail
Unit 1
Sarnia, ONT

Dear Mr. Hurricane:

RE: Hurricane v. Hurricane

I am writing to confirm the instructions you
gave to me at our meeting on Monday, March
3rd, 1986, at the offices of Scarlet, Rose
and Indigo.

At our meeting I explained to you that I
believed the settlement proposal made by
your wife was extremely close to an award
she could expect a judge to make, should
this matter go to trial, under the Family
Law Act. I explained to you that I thought
some small adjustments could be made to the
terms proposed and we discussed those.
After our discussion, you instructed me to
proceed with negotiations with your wife's
lawyer, Ms. Bonnie Scooter. I have set out
those instructions in what follows.[20]

The Condominium

You have instructed me to agree to
transferring title of the condominium from
your name to your name and your wife's as
tenants-in-common. I have explained to you
that the legal effect of sharing title with

---

[20]   " . . . in this letter."

your wife as a tenant in common is, among other things, that you can will your half of the property as you see fit.

You advised me in our meeting that you have listed the property with a real estate agent, Manfred Strange. You authorized me to disclose this fact to Ms. Scooter in the hope that this would encourage a quick resolution of the matter.

Division of Other Property

Your wife's lawyer has proposed settling the division of the balance of the property with a payment of $11,000 to your wife before July 31st, 1986.[21] You and I[22] have calculated the value of these assets and any liabilities and reached the conclusion that your wife's share has a value of approximately $5,000 to $7,000. you have instructed me to negotiate a reduction in the figure of $11,000. In addition, you have instructed me to negotiate a change in the date by which payment has been made. I shall attempt to extend this date to Thanksgiving 1986.

In my view,[23] given your present circumstances and those of your wife, maintenance in the amount of $600 a month is not unreasonable. You have agreed with this

---

[21] It is not clear in this sentence just who is doing the paying. Of course, it is presumably the client but never presume. I would rewrite it

> Your wife's lawyer has proposed settling the division of the balance of the property with your payment to your wife of $11,000 before July 31, 1986.

This specifies that the client is paying his wife.

[22] Compare how clear this is with the two ambiguous cases of "we" in the last letter.

[23] "In my view" is an unnecessary phrase. It's the author's letter so it had better be the author's view.

assessment. I understand that when you sell the condominium, you will no longer be operating your business and your circumstances will be drastically changed. Given this, in my view,[24] it is reasonable that your obligation to pay support of $600/month end when you have sold the condominium. You have instructed me to negotiate this provision. You instructed me to negotiate this term knowing that it could be quite some time before the condominium is sold and there is an end to the maintenance payments.

OHIP

It is your understanding that your wife has no intention[25] of returning to Ontario. In view of this,[26] you do not think it is reasonable that you continue to pay OHIP premiums on her behalf. You have instructed me to negotiate an end to these payments on your wife's behalf.[27]

I trust the foregoing accurately sets out your instructions to me. If there is an error, I hope that you will advise me.[28]

I confirm[29] before I am able to proceed with the negotiations, I will require[30] a further

---

[24]   "I think" would do.

[25]   This is a classic verb turned into a noun. ". . . your wife does not intend to return . . . ."

[26]   "And" would be a much shorter link between these two ideas. "It is your understanding that your wife does not intend to return to Ontario and you do not think it is reasonable that you continue to pay OHIP premiums on her behalf."

[27]   Delete "on your wife's behalf." It is both redundant and confusing. It sounds a bit as if the author of the letter is negotiating on the wife's behalf.

[28]   All of a sudden, the author has switched from businesslike to stuffy. "If I have misunderstood your instructions, please call me immediately."

retainer [31] of $250. You have advised me that
a cheque in that amount will be sent to
Scarlett, Rose and Indigo early in the week
of March 3rd, 1986.

I will report to you on the progress of the
settlement negotiations. [32]

                              Yours very truly,

                              MATILDA INDIGO

P.S. I acknowledge receipt of your cheque in
the amount of $250 on March 7th, 1986. [33]

---

[29]   "As I mentioned" would do nicely for this. There's no need to
be stuffy or reticent about money. It's part of the business.

[30]   "need"

[31]   Most people are not sure what a "retainer" is. "Payment"
would be better.

[32]   Again, I prefer a more relaxed "let you know" over the stuffier
"report." "I will let you know when there is progress on the
settlement negotiations." It reduces the client's tension level
when the letter is warm and friendly while still being
professional. If you were a doctor, it would be called good
bedside manner. Lawyers need good deskside manner.

[33]   Come on. Who talks like that? Just say what you mean and
don't forget to say "Thank-you" when the nice people pay their
bills. "We received you cheque for $250 on March 7th.
Thanks."

LETTER #3 -
YOU'RE FIRED

As you may figure out from the fact that my comments on the next letter are longer than the letter, it's a letter that is in serious trouble.

The primary problem is the author has presumed that the reader will have everything fresh in her mind. Instead, he needs to *ensure* that everything is fresh in her mind by putting it there.

Alpha, Bravo, Delta and Foxtrot
Barristers and Solicitors
123 Any Street
Toronto, Ontario

July 15, 1983

Ms. Matilda Smith
999 South Drive
Agincourt, ONT

Dear Ms. Smith:

RE: Smith ats Jones
        Our file: 000-1

Further to our telephone conversation of July 16, 1983, we confirm your instructions to offer to Mr. Jones the following amounts in settlement of his claim: [34]

1.   Gross bi-monthly [35] pay in the amount of $1,750.00 less withholding tax at 27% which amounts to a net payment of $1,220,00. [36]

---

[34]   This letter makes a fatal mistake: it presumes too much. Remember that letters like this have at least two audiences, both the client and anyone else (like another lawyer) reading the file. This letter *might* be OK for the client since she was in on the meeting, but not for anyone else. It wasn't until I read the next letter that I was able to make sense out of this one.

On this first paragraph, I don't like "further to" openings. Here is an option.

This letter is to confirm the instruction you gave me over the telephone this morning.

You have instructed us to offer Mr. Jones the following amounts in settlement of his claim.

[35]   The author exhibits the common but inexcusable confusion over the meaning of "bi-monthly." The prefix *bi* means *two* so bi-monthly is once every two months. The prefix *semi* means *half* so semi-monthly means twice a month. Here, I believe the author meant "semi-monthly" pay of $1,750, a more reasonable amount, even in the 1980s when this was originally written. Of course, neither bi-monthly nor semi-monthly is the same as once ever two weeks (bi-weekly or

2.   Payment on account of Mr. Jones' variable quarterly objective for the months of April, May and June in the amount of $383.00 which represents a gross payment of $524.75 less withholding tax of $141.75.[37]

We have advised the solicitors for Mr. Jones that the computer division has not shown a profit and therefore none of the employees including his client are entitled to any amount on account of profit sharing.[38]

We shall keep you advised.[39]

Yours very truly,

ALPHA, BRAVO
DELTA AND FOXTROT

---

fortnightly) yet, in the next letter, this same author refers to this money as "two weeks salary." Which is it supposed to be?

[36]   Actually, no it doesn't. $1750 less 27% is *not* $1220 but $1277.50. This is the kind of error that should be picked up on a truth and accuracy revision. If I had received this letter, I would wonder about the competence of the lawyer with whom I was dealing.

[37]   This paragraph is unclear about just what is being offered here. Again, you have to refer to the next letter (the actual settlement offer) to understand exactly what the author is trying to say. I'd redo it this way:

> 2. Five percent of Mr. Jones' quarterly salary as settlement of his claim for a bonus based on his "variable quarterly objective." This amounts to $524.75. Subtract withholding of $141.75 and there's a net payment of $383.00.

[38]   This paragraph is actually part three of the settlement offer. It's not a question of what you have told (not "advised") the other lawyers but what you have been instructed to offer. So, its style should match the other elements in the offer.

> 3. Nothing for profit sharing as the computer division has not shown a profit.

[39]   A short action list would be nice here letting the reader know exactly what the lawyer is going to do and when. It has the side benefit of making the lawyer aware of just what he is gong to do and when.

LETTER #4 -
BUT WE DIDN'T MEAN IT

This letter suffers mostly from poor organization. Each topic (pay, bonus, profit sharing) is addressed twice in different parts of the letter. It would be better to deal with each once them summarize the offer at the end.

I have edited the existing letter. However, what this letter needs most is a rethink and a rewrite, not just an edit. The rewrite is the next letter in the examples.

Alpha, Bravo, Delta and Foxtrot

Barristers and Solicitors
123 Any Street
Toronto, ONT

WITHOUT PREJUDICE

Mr. S.V.P. Brown
Brown, White and Black
Barristers and Solicitors
Suite 1000
23000 Yonge Street
Willowdale, ONT

Dear Sirs:

RE: Smith ats Jones
       Our file: 000-1

Further to your letter of June 17, 1983,[40] and our response of July 2, 1983,[41] we have now had and opportunity to review the circumstances surrounding your client's employment and his dismissal.

Your client was employed by Smith and Company Inc., computer division, for just over 4 months. Mr. Jones' dismissal was on account of company wide lay-offs within the computer division. My client advised that the total nation wide staff of the computer

---

[40]   A date in this format requires a comma after the year: ". . . of June 17, 1983, and our . . . ." As a very crude rule of thumb, commas move in pairs. You need the first comma to distinguish the day from the year. The second comma balances the first comma.

You would not need a comma if the date is in the format "17 June 1983" nor do you need a comma in the expression "June 1983."

[41]   Break the sentence here by adding the words "This letter is" to the beginning of the sentence. It would turn out like this:

This letter is further to your letter of June 17, 1983, and our response of July 2, 1983. We have now had an opportunity . . . ."

~~division was reduced from 40 employees to 30
employees and~~ There were 40 employees in the
division. Mr. Jones was one of ~~the~~ 10
employees laid-off.

~~Our client advised that~~ Mr. Jones received
two weeks pay in lieu of notice. ~~We are
further advised that Mr. Jones~~ He was
offered and took advantage of Drake's
executive search services which were
provided to him upon his dismissal as a
courtesy.[42]

With respect to your claim for profit
sharing, ~~we advise that~~ the computer
division has not shown a profit since its
inception two years ago. Consequently, none
of the employees in the computer division
have received ~~any amounts on account of~~
profit sharing payments. ~~and~~ accordingly,
your client is not entitled to any ~~amounts
up~~ payments for the period to the end of
November 1983 as ~~stated in your demand
letter~~ you demanded.

~~With respect to the bonus you claim is due
to your client, we advise as follows.~~ You
claim your client is entitled to a bonus.
He is not. For each quarter ~~of the year
worked,~~ if an employee meets his sales
objective, he receives 10% of his salary for
that quarter as a bonus. ~~Our client's
policy is that~~ this bonus, called a variable
quarterly objective, is calculated at the
end of each quarter. ~~and that~~ in order to
qualify for the bonus, an employee must
~~still~~ be an employee at the end of that
particular quarter. The last quarter that
Mr. Jones was employed with our client
~~concluded at the end of March 1983~~ ended
March 31, 198_3_. The next quarter ~~in~~ for

---

[42]   Invert these last two phrases: " . . . which were provided to him
        as a courtesy upon his dismissal." Otherwise, you are saying
        that his dismissal was a courtesy.

which the bonus ~~is~~ was calculated ~~consists~~ consisted of the months of April, May and June. ~~and~~ as of the end of June, Mr. Jones was not employed by our client.[43]

~~Further to the above information,~~ we have received instructions from our client to make the following offer of settlement on a without prejudice basis: [44]

1.   Two weeks salary, less ~~the appropriate~~ withholding tax. Mr. Jones' gross salary for two weeks was $1,750.00. The net salary after tax is ~~$1,220.00~~ $1277.50.[45] Since your client has already received two weeks salary in lieu of notice, the additional two weeks results in your client ~~having received~~ receiving the equivalent of one month notice.

2.   ~~Pursuant to our client's policies,~~ Mr. Jones is not entitled to any bonus. However, ~~our client advises that~~ for the last quarter (April, May and June) Mr. Jones obtained 50% of his variable quarterly objective. An employee is normally paid 10% of his salary for the last quarter if he obtains a 100% variable quarterly objective.

---

[43] The original version of the paragraph contained 135 words in five sentences. The average length was 27 words. The edit is 116 words in eight sentences, average length 14.5 words. Here's the revised paragraph.

> You claim your client is entitled to a bonus. He is not. For each quarter if an employee meets his sales objective, he receives 10% of his salary for that quarter as a bonus. This bonus, called a variable quarterly objective, is calculated at the end of each quarter. In order to qualify for the bonus, an employee must be an employee at the end of that particular quarter. The last quarter that Mr. Jones was employed with our client ended March 31, 1986. The next quarter in which the bonus is calculated consists of the months of April, May and June. As of the end of June, Mr. Jones was not employed by our client.

[44] An offer is just an offer. It never prejudices you.

[45] See notes number 26 and 27.

Since Mr. Jones obtained 50% of his variable quarterly objective, ~~he is entitled~~ [46] Smith & Company is offering 5% of his salary for the last quarter. This amounts to a net variable quarterly objective of $383.00 based on a gross payment of $524.75 less withholding tax of $141.75. ~~Therefore, in addition to the additional salary referred to above, our client is prepared to also make the variable quarterly objective payment of $383.00 (after tax).~~ [47]

3.   Your client is not entitled to any ~~amounts on account of~~ payment for profit sharing ~~for the reasons outlined above~~ since the computer division has no profit to share.

Yours truly,

ALPHA, BRAVO,
DELTA AND FOXTROT

---

[46]   Do you really want to say he is "entitled" to this. Your client will pay it as a good will gesture. I don't think you ever want to say he is entitled to it.

[47]   This entire closing section is redundant.

REWRITE NOTES

I've rewritten the previous letter starting on the next page.

The rewrite accomplishes several things. First, it clarifies what is being offered and why. Second, it does a little selling. After all, you have to sell this offer to Mr. Jones and his lawyer. That's part of your job.

I've shortened it by a quarter (407 vs. 559 words) and also simplified the language substantially. I analyzed the two letters using the Flesch-Kinkaid readability index which indicates the level of education a reader would need to understand the letter easily. The original letter required a grade 12 education. The rewrite comes in at a grade 8 level.

Notice, too, that I have not used the word "advise" in any of its forms even once. Lawyers advise their clients as to the best course of action. Clients "inform" or "tell" their lawyers what the facts are and "instruct" them to do things. Lawyers "inform" and "tell" other lawyers things.

Alpha, Bravo, Delta and Foxtrot
Barristers and Solicitors
123 Any Street
Toronto, ONT

WITHOUT PREJUDICE

Mr. S.V.P. Brown
Brown, White and Black
Barristers and Solicitors
Suite 1000
23000 Yonge Street
Willowdale, ONT

Dear Mr. Brown,[48]

RE: Smith ats Jones
       Our file: 000-1

Dear Sirs:

This letter is in response to your letter of
June 17, 1983, and supplements our response
of July 2, 1983. We have now had an
opportunity to review the circumstances
surrounding your client's employment with
Smith and Company and his dismissal. Our
information is based on discussions with Ms.
Matilda Smith of Smith and Company.[49]

PAY IN LIEU OF NOTICE[50]

The computer division of Smith and Company
employed Mr. Jones for just over four
months. Out of forty employees in the
division, he was one of ten laid off.

---

[48]   This is to the lawyer handling the file so make it to him, not
       "Dear Sirs."

[49]   This introduction settles the reader's mind onto the topic and
       lets him adjust his thinking to the topic at hand.

[50]   Headings like this help keep the reader on track.

He was given two weeks pay in lieu of notice. He was offered and took advantage of Drakes Executive Search Services at company expense.

Smith and Company is prepared to offer a further two weeks' pay, meaning Mr. Jones will have received a month's notice after four months employment. Two weeks' pay is $1750 gross less withholding tax of $472.50 leaving a net payment of $1277.50.

BONUS

Your client is claiming a sales bonus under the company's "variable quarterly objective" policy. However, he does not qualify for one.

The Smith and Company policy is that if a sales employee meets his variable quarterly objective, a sales quota that varies from quarter to quarter, he receives a bonus of 10% of his salary for that quarter. However, to qualify, an employee must still be working for the company as of the end of the quarter. Mr. Jones was not working for the company at the end of the second quarter of 1983 and so does not qualify for a bonus.

Nonetheless, the company is willing to recognize Mr. Smith's efforts. As he had achieved 50% of his variable quarterly objective for the second quarter of 1983, the company is willing to pay him half the bonus. That's 5% of his quarterly salary or $524.75 less withholding tax of $141.75 for a net payment of $383.00.

PROFIT SHARING

The computer division of Smith and Company has not shown a profit since its inception two years ago. Therefore, the company is not willing to offer any payment for profit sharing. No employees of the division have received profit sharing payments.

SUMMARY

So, Smith and Company is willing to offer Mr. Jones:

(a)   a additional two weeks pay in lieu of notice;

(g)   a bonus payment equal to 5% of his quarterly salary;

(c)   nothing for profit sharing.

Please let me know if this offer is acceptable.

Regards,

ALPHA, BRAVO, DELTA AND FOXTROT

FACTUM

The function of a factum or brief is to persuade. This factum is not particularly persuasive. Read it over, bearing in mind the words of Justice Bablitch of the Wisconsin Supreme Court:

> Effective brief writing requires that you constantly remind yourself for whom it is you are writing. You are not writing to impress your client with the depth of your intellect. You are writing for the judge. He or she is your sole audience.
>
> Your role is to persuade, not to impress. When the desire to impress becomes more important that the desire to persuade, it can lead to awful results. In an attempt to be eloquent, intellectual and erudite, the unfortunate result all to frequently is legalese and legal jargon put in a form called a legal brief.[1]

---

[1] William A. Bablitch, "Writing to Win," The Compleat Lawyer, Winter 1988.

IN THE SUPREME COURT OF ONTARIO

The Green Bank

vs.

ABC Company and John Smith

**FACTUM OF THE PLAINTIFF
THE GREEN BANK**

PART I - NATURE OF THE PROCEEDINGS

1.   The Plaintiff, the Green Bank, seeks the following relief: [2]

(a)   an Order pursuant to Rule 21.01(1)(b) striking out the Statement of Defence of John Smith on the ground that it discloses no reasonable defence;

(b)   in the alternative, an Order pursuant to Rule 25.11 striking out certain paragraphs in the Statement of Defence as being scandalous, frivolous or

---

[2]   Starting with the details of the relief you are seeking strikes me as a bit strange. What you are trying to do in this section is let the court know, in general terms, what kind of proceedings are at hand. This is a motion to strike a Statement of Defence so that's all you need in the first paragraph. The details of the relief you are seeking can wait until the end.

If you are going to stick with this format, then I would suggest rewriting the paragraphs relating to the specific relief.

1.   The Plaintiff, the Green Bank, seeks the following relief:

(a)   an Order under Rule 21.01(1)(b) striking out the Statement of Defence of John Smith. It discloses no reasonable defence.

(b)   Alternatively, an Order under Rule 25.11 striking out sections of the Statement of Defence. These sections are scandalous, frivolous or vexatious and prejudice and delay the fair trial of this case.

vexatious and as prejudicing and delaying the fair trial of the action;

(c) in the alternative, an Order pursuant to Rule 25.10 for particulars with respect to certain allegations in the Statement of Defence of John Smith, which particulars are set out in Schedule "A" attached hereto; [3]

(d) in the alternative, an Order extending the time within which to deliver a Reply; and

(e) such further and other relief as this honorable court may deem just. [4]

PART II - THE FACTS

2. The major allegations made by the Plaintiff, the Green Bank ("The Bank"), against the Defendant, John Smith ("Smith") appear in paragraphs 5 and 7 of the Statement of Claim. [5] The Bank claims:

---

[3] Paragraph 1(c) has some problems. It asks for particulars about certain allegations then says those particulars are set out in Schedule "A." Obviously this is a mistake but a cursory proof reading let it get out the door at the firm that actually filed this factum. At the least, its embarrassing, at the most it could cost something.

> (c) Alternatively, an Order under Rule 25.10 for particulars about certain allegations in the Statement of Defence of John Smith. These allegations are set out in Schedule "A" of this factum.

[4] Paragraph 1(e) is not necessary in Ontario (where this factum was filed) and in many other jurisdictions. The Rules give the court the power to grant all forms of relief allowed even when they are not specifically requested.

The rules were rewritten in many jurisdictions to do away with the need for this paragraph in order to simplify _ and shorten _ pleadings. Yet many, even most lawyers, still include this line. Read the rules in your jurisdiction and find out if it is really needed.

[5] Why has the author waited until here to specify the short forms "The Bank" and "Smith"? Why not put them when the parties are first mentioned? That's where they belong.

(i) The Defendant Company is indebted to the Bank by virtue of an overdraft in the amount of $3,124.06 U.S. funds;[6]

(ii) The Defendant, Smith, signed an unlimited written guarantee whereby he guaranteed to the bank payment and discharge of all liabilities to the Bank of the Defendant Company.[7]

3. The Defendant Smith denies in line 4 of his Statement of Defence that an unlimited guarantee was given. The Defendant, Smith, appears to assert in the last paragraph of his Statement of Defence a Counter claim against the Bank and claims:[8]

(a) restitution for financial losses suffered in the amount of $150,000.00; and

(b) damages for personal and professional destruction of reputation and credit standing in the community resulting from the charges of criminal fraud. The Defendant asks the sum of $150,000.00.[9]

---

[6] In 2(i), specify who the defendant company is by name since it is only mentioned twice. Simplify the language.

ABC Company owes the Bank $3,124.06 U.S. funds under an overdraft.

Also, why is this 2(i) and not 2(a), the style used under the other paragraphs?

[7] 2(ii) needs some editing as well.

Smith signed an unlimited written guarantee. In it he guaranteed to discharge all of ABC's debts to the Bank if ABC did not.

[8] Paragraph 3 should be split in two with appropriate renumbering of the rest of the paragraphs. The first sentence concerns Smith's defence. The second sentence concerns his counterclaim. They do not belong in the same paragraph.

[9] It is not clear whether Smith is asking for $150,000 restitution *and* $150,000 damages or for a total of $150,000.

Also, the last sentence in paragraph 3(b) says, "The defendant asks the sum of $150,000." You ask *for* a sum.

4.   The ABC Company has not delivered a
Statement of Defence to the action herein.[10]

PART III - THE LAW

5.   The Statement of Defence contravenes
Rule 21.01(1)(b) and discloses no reasonable
defence in that there are no particulars to
inform the Plaintiff of the basis upon which
it is alleged that the Defendant is not
liable pursuant to the guarantee.[11]   The
pleading is so defective, inadequate and
contains so much irrelevant matter that it
should be struck out rather than amended.[12]

---

[10]   Replace "herein" with "in this action" or "in this case."

[11]   You must always fight a lawyer's (un)natural tendency to write
long sentences. The usual excuse offered is that there are all
these conditions that need to be in the same sentence. They
don't. Perhaps in the same paragraph but not the same
sentence. For example, at the beginning of paragraph 5, the
first very long sentence (40 words) can be divided into two
shorter ones of 12 and 26 with no loss of clarity.

> The Statement of Defence contravenes Rule
> 21.01(1)(b) and discloses no reasonable defence.
> There are no particulars to inform the Plaintiff of the
> basis upon which it is alleged that the Defendant is
> not liable pursuant to he guarantee.

A good rule of thumb is to strive for sentences of fewer than
fifteen words and paragraphs of no more than five sentences.

Even when cut in half, the first sentence is still unclear.
Presuming that Rule 21.01(1)(b) is the rule that says you can
strike out a Statement of Defence that does not disclose a
defence, the sentence says, "The Statement of Defence
discloses no reasonable defence and discloses no reasonable
defence." Instead, say,

> The Statement of Defence discloses no reasonable
> defence (Rule 21.01(1)(b)). It does not say why Smith
> is not liable under his guarantee.

[12]   This sentence belongs in another paragraph. It does not relate
directly to the previous sentence. The case law is the
authority for that statement, not R. 21.01(1)(b).

Admittedly, the audience for this particular piece of writing is
a judge who probably knows the rules, but he or she might
have just come to the bench from 20 years in criminal law.
The judge may not have looked at the rules of court since law

---

E. & S. Carpentry Contractors Ltd. v.
Fedak, et al, (1981), 18 CPC 307 (Ont.
H.C.)

Guetta v. The Queen, (1975), 17 C.P.R.
(2nd) 31 (Fed. Ct.);

6.   The Statement of Defence and
Counterclaim may prejudice or delay the fair
trial of the action and therefore is
scandalous, frivolous and vexatious within
the meaning of Rule 25.11 of the Rules of
Civil Procedure [13] as the said[14] pleading
lacks particularity [15] and is filled with
irrelevant and prejudicial allegations.[16]

Brumskill v. Huttenville Farm Labour
Cooperative Ltd., [1953] O.W.N. 564
(Ont.H.C.)

7.   A pleading which raises an issue, the
determination of which can have no effect
upon the outcome of the action, is
embarrassing and should be struck out.[17]

---

school. Never make presumptions about the knowledge of
your audience.

[13]   Paragraph 6 suddenly starts talking about the Rules of Civil
Procedure. Up until now we've heard only about the Rules.
Why the sudden formality? Or are these different Rules?

[14]   Drop "said"; "the pleading" is fine.

[15]   Few of us use the word "particuarity" in everyday speech.
Instead, we speak of "details" That is a better word to use
here.

[16]   Overall, it makes more sense to reverse the order of the
information in this paragraph and break it up into several
sentences.

The Statement of Defence lacks details. It is filled
with irrelevant and prejudicial allegations. As a
result, it is "scandalous, frivolous and vexatious"
under rule 25.11 and may delay or prejudice the fair
trial of this case.

[17]   Paragraph 7 is confusing. It says that embarrassing pleadings
in general can be struck out but makes no claim that the
Statement of Defence at hand is embarrassing and should be
struck.

<u>Everdale Place</u> v. <u>Rimmer, et al</u>,
(1975), 8 O.R. (2nd) 641 (H.C.)

8.   It is the duty of the Court to
criticize [18] the pleadings from the point of
view of intelligibility and compliance with
the Rules.

<u>Steiner</u> v. <u>Lindzon, et al</u>, (1976) 14
O.R. (2nd) 122 (H.C.)

<u>Cadillac Contracting and Developments
Ltd.</u> v. <u>Tannenbaum</u>, [1954] O.W.N. 221
(H.C.);

<u>Dolgy</u> v. <u>Shelter</u>, [1949] O.W.N. 545
(H.C.)

9.   Where [19] particulars are extensive and
will cause difficulty and inconvenience in
understanding the Defendant's claim, the
should be embodied in a new Statement of
Defence. [20]

<u>Hammell</u> v. <u>B.A. Oil Company</u> [1945]
O.W.N. 660 (H.C.)

---

[18]   This is passive. Change it to the active voice: "The Court has a
duty to criticize. . . ."

[19]   "Where" is not correct. "Where" refers to physical location.
The word the author wants is "when."

[20]   Again, reverse the order of the information. What should be
done under what circumstances.

The Defendant's should file a new Statement of
Defence if their particulars are extensive and will
make it difficult and inconvenient to understand the
Defendant's claim.

PART IV – ORDER REQUESTED

10.   The Plaintiff therefore seeks an Order in accordance with paragraph 1 of this Factum.[21]

ALL OF WHICH IS RESPECTFULLY SUBMITTED [22]

---

[21]   This section refers back to the beginning. However, as I said before, I think the plea for relief belongs here. Take a look at the way I've handled this section in the rewrite.

[22]   This style of closing is archaic and unnecessary. Why not "Submitted by Perrin and Company, Solicitors for the Green Bank."

FACTUM REWRITE

Ultimately, good writing requires more than just editing. The original factum is a decent first draft but the author has been sloppy. What it needs most is a thorough rewrite.

I've tried to "punch up" the factum a bit, using simpler language and injecting a bit of salesmanship. After all, I want to persuade the judge to trash this case before it can even get to trial. I can't just go through the motions. I have to make him or her believe that the other side is so incompetent and specious they shouldn't be given a chance to even argue their case in court. That's going to run against a judge's grain so I have to do a lot of convincing here.

IN THE SUPREME COURT OF ONTARIO

The Green Bank

vs.

ABC Company and John Smith

FACTUM OF THE PLAINTIFF
THE GREEN BANK

I - NATURE OF THE PROCEEDINGS

1.   The Plaintiff in this action, the Green Bank
("the Bank"), wishes the Court to strike out the
Statement of Defence of the Defendant John Smith
("Smith") or to provide other relief.

II - THE FACTS

2.   In brief, ABC Company owes the Bank
$3,124.06 U.S. funds by virtue of an overdraft.
Smith signed an unlimited written guarantee
promising to pay the debts of ABC Company to the
Bank. (These allegations against Smith are in
paragraphs 5 and 7 of the Statement of Claim.)

3.   Smith denies that he signed an unlimited
guarantee (line 4 of his Statement of Defence).

4.   In the last paragraph of his Statement of
Defence, Smith appears to counterclaim against the
Bank for a total of $300,000. He claims $150,000
for financial losses he has suffered and another
$150,000 for destruction of his personal and
professional reputations and of his credit rating
as a result of charges of criminal fraud which he
currently faces.

5.   The ABC Company has not delivered a
Statement of Defence.

III - THE LAW

6.   Smith's Statement of Defence should be
struck out on the grounds that it discloses no
reasonable defence (Rule 21.01(1)(b)). It says
Smith is not liable to the Bank but provides no

details as to <u>why</u> he is not liable. The Statement is so defective and inadequate and it contains so much irrelevant material that it should be struck out rather than amended.

> <u>E. & S. Carpentry Contractors Ltd.</u> v. <u>Fedak, et al</u>, (1981), 18 CPC 307 (Ont. H.C.)
>
> <u>Guetta</u> v. <u>The Queen</u>, (1975), 17 C.P.R. (2nd) 31 (Fed. Ct.)

7.   The Statement of Defence also contains irrelevant and prejudicial allegations which may prejudice or delay the fair trial of this action. Therefore, it is "scandalous, frivolous and vexatious" under Rule 25.11 and should be struck out.

> <u>Brumskill</u> v. <u>Huttenville Farm Labour Cooperative Ltd.</u>, [1953] O.W.N. 564 (Ont.H.C.)

8.   The Statement of Defence raises irrelevant issues. Therefore it is "embarrassing" and should be struck out.

> <u>Everdale Place</u> v. <u>Rimmer, et al</u>, (1975), 8 O.R. (2nd) 641 (H.C.)

9.   The Court has a duty to criticize the intelligibility of the pleadings and their compliance with the Rules and should therefore grant the Bank the relief it seeks.

> <u>Steiner</u> v. <u>Lindzon, et al</u>, (1976) 14 O.R. (2nd) 122 (H.C.)
>
> <u>Cadillac Contracting and Developments Ltd.</u> v. <u>Tannenbaum</u>, [1954] O.W.N. 221 (H.C.);
>
> <u>Dolgy</u> v. <u>Shelter</u>, [1949] O.W.N. 545 (H.C.)

10.   Should the Court decide that the Defendant should be allowed to provide details, the Bank argues they should take the form of a new Statement of Defence. The details requested are extensive. Attempting to incorporate them into the existing Statement of Defence will make it difficult and inconvenient to understand.

Hammell v. B.A. Oil Company [1945] O.W.N. 660 (H.C.)

IV – RELIEF SOUGHT

The Bank asks the Court to grant the following relief.

a.   An Order under Rule 20.01(1)(b) striking out the Smith's Statement of Defence on the ground that it discloses no reasonable defence.

b.   Alternatively, an Order under Rule 25.11 striking out parts of the Statement of Defence for being scandalous, frivolous or vexatious and for prejudicing and delaying the fair trial of this action.

c.   Alternatively, an Order under Rule 25.10 directing Smith to provide details of certain allegations in his Statement of Defence. (The allegations concerned are listed in Schedule A, attached.)

d.   Alternatively, an Order extending the time in which the Bank may reply to the Statement of Defence.

SUBMITTED BY PERRIN AND COMPANY,
SOLICITORS FOR THE GREEN BANK

CONTRACTS

With rare exceptions, a nonprofessional should be able to pick up any piece of legal drafting and almost instantly know what it is. When a lawyer has to read virtually an entire document just to figure out what it is trying to do—and I did—you know something is wrong.

The contract on the next few pages is a typical example of contract drafting. In other words, it is completely unintelligible to anyone without a law degree, and even we have to work at it a bit. It contains at least one example of almost everything that is wrong with legal writing.

First, read it through and follow my comments as I point out each of the problem areas.

There are then two redrafts. The first attempts to merely translate it into English while retaining the original organization. The second redraft attempts to find the core of the agreement and produce a contract that the parties can understand. What is really going on here? What kinds of right/responsibilities/relationship are we trying to create?

I've included more comments before each of these redrafts.

AGREEMENT [1]

BETWEEN:

ABC Real Estate Corporation

The "Landlord"

AND

Joe's Pizza, Limited

The "Tenant"

WHEREAS [2] the Landlord is the owner [3] of a building located on lands municipally known as 123 Main Street, in the City of Toronto in the Province of Ontario [4] (the "Building");

AND WHEREAS [5] pursuant to an agreement dated as of July 10, 1987 [6] (the "Agreement"), [7] the

---

[1]   As I said, a nonprofessional should be able to understand what he or she is reading right from the beginning. Here, the title is too vague. I suggest "Consent to Encumbrance."

[2]   Notice how I've handled the recitals in the second rewrite. The function of recitals is to provide the parties (the primary audience) and a Court (the secondary audience) with the background necessary to understand the contract. That's all. They're not an exercise in archaic English construction.

[3]   This is a verb (to own) turned into a noun. Use the verb. "The Landlord owns . . . ."

[4]   ". . . in the Country of Canada, in the Northern Hemisphere of the Planet of Earth in the Star System of Sol in the Galaxy Milky Way." Come on! The idea is to identify the property concerned clearly and unambiguously. "The Landlord owns a building at 123 Main Street, Toronto, Ontario" would do just fine. As far as we know, there's only one building in the entire universe with that address.

[5]   This paragraph and the next four are really irrelevant. All that matters is that the Landlord and Tenant have that relationship

Landlord agreed to lease to the Tenant and the Tenant agreed to lease from the Landlord certain premises within the Building [8] (the "Leased Premises") for an interim period of time as described in the Agreement (the "Interim Period");

AND WHEREAS the Tenant has covenanted and agreed [9] with the landlord that throughout the Interim Period, the Tenant shall be bound by the terms, covenants, conditions and agreements [10] provided for in a form of lease, said form of lease attached as Schedule "C" to the Agreement (the "Form of Lease"), subject to changes made necessary by the Agreement;

AND WHEREAS the Agreement and Form of Lease both provide covenants and agreements which must be observed and performed by the parties;

---

now. We don't really care how they there. All this talk about an interim agreement and a form of lease is a waste of time. If there is every litigation over this contract, the facts will all come out anyway. All the documents will be filed. It's not necessary to tell all of it here.

6   What is "dated as of"? Is that the effective date? The signing date? The drafting date?

There are two important dates with a contract: the date it is signed and, if it is different, the date on which it comes (came) into force. There may be others depending on the details of the deal, but the critical ones are those two.

7   That fact that you're going to refer to another document as the "Agreement" is yet another reason to title this document something other than simply "Agreement." But then, that one should have been called "Lease," shouldn't it?

8   After all the specificity about the location of the building, now all of a sudden the author is content with "certain premises within the building." That could be the whole building or just a closet. Certainly a suite number would not be out of line here.

9   The difference between a contract and covenant was abolished a long time ago. "Agreed" would do just fine.

10   Freight train. "Agreements" or "terms" would be sufficient.

AND WHEREAS pursuant to the Agreement, upon expiration of the Interim Period,[11] the Landlord has agreed to continue to lease to the Tenant and the Tenant has agreed to continue to lease from the Landlord the Leased Premises upon the terms and conditions set out in the Agreement as amended by the Form of Lease for a term of five (5)[12] years commencing on the "Permanent Lease Commencement Date", as such term is defined in the Agreement;

AND WHEREAS [13] the Tenant has requested pursuant to the Agreement and Form of Lease, that the Landlord consent to a certain deed of trust and mortgage (the "Trust Deed") between the Tenant and ABC Trust Company ("Trust"), said Trust Deed to bear formal date of the 30th day of May, 1987; [14]

AND WHEREAS certain provisions of the Trust Deed purport to provide Trust with priority over the rights of the Landlord, such rights provided for under the Agreement and Form of Lease (the "Landlord's Rights").[15]

---

[11] This is a verb turned into a noun. "When the Interim Period expires . . . ."

[12] Why both? What if you accidentally but "five (50)"? Which one counts? You're just asking to make a mistake. Say it only once and say it right.

[13] Now we're back to something relevant. The Tenant wants to encumber some property over which the Landlord has first call.

[14] What the heck is a "formal date"? The date on which it was formed? Executed? Effective? Or is a date just pulled from the air?

[15] If you are going to embark on the great "Whereas" and semicolon kind of construction, you should at least be consistent. That means this is not the end of the sentence. You've said, "Whereas A, and Whereas B." Sorry, you've got to continue trying to construct an entire contract in a single sentence.

Now, obviously, that is ridiculous. Why not use simple, short sentences?

NOW THEREFORE WITNESSETH THAT: [16]

1.   The Landlord hereby consents, subject to the qualification provided for in paragraph 2 herein,[17] to the Tenant to encumber the Tenant's property found on the Leased Premises in the manner provided for [18] by the Trust Deed on condition [19] that one photocopy of the executed Trust Deed is provided to the Landlord's solicitors within two weeks of execution of the said Trust Deed.

2.   Notwithstanding [20] any other provision herein,[21] the Landlord does not consent and shall in no circumstances [22] be deemed to have consented to those provisions contained in the Trust Deed which in any manner whatsoever,[23] would have a negative impact upon the Landlord's Rights including, without restricting the generality of the

---

[16]   Totally archaic form. A contract has three parts: recitals (the background and history necessary to understand the contract), the agreements themselves and the execution. So, why not use titles like that.

[17]   Of course it's subject to paragraph 2. The contract must be read as a whole. Therefore, you can drop this qualification.

[18]   The placement of the phrase "in the manner provided for" makes it modify "found": ". . . the tenants property found . . . in the manner provided . . . ." When you try to construct a 62 word sentence, you run into those kinds of problems. Break this behemoth up. My first rewrite cuts it in thirds.

[19]   Same problem. "On condition" also modifies "found." Modifiers modify the most recent word or phrase they can modify. Keep your modifier next to what they modify. If your sentences are short, that's a lot easier to do.

[20]   One of the great old chestnuts of legal drafting. Also completely out of date. Try "In spite of."

[21]   Use "in this agreement."

[22]   Use "not" for "in no circumstances." Not is about as absolute as you can get.

[23]   Drop "whatsoever." "In any manner" covers the waterfront. *Any* means *any.*

forgoing,[24] provisions found in Articles III, IV, VI, VII, VIII and IX of the Trust Deed which purport to limit the Landlord's Rights to:

    (a)   distrain for non-payment of rent;

    (b)   recover accelerated rent;

    (c)   enforce a lien on all stock-in-trade, inventory, fixtures, equipment or facilities[25] of the Tenant in the event of default;

    (d)   enforce any right with respect to insurance;

    (e)   re-enter and/or re-let the leased premises or avail itself to other such remedies in the event of default; or

    (f)   recover from the Tenant any property owned by the Tenant and charged under the Trust Deed when the Tenant desires[26] to deal with such property in a manner disadvantageous to the Landlord.

3.   This consent shall be construed in accordance with and governed by the laws of the Province of Ontario[27] and shall extend to

---

[24]   "Includes" already does not restrict the generality of the foregoing. That is the meaning of "includes." The rule of interpretation that says a list is all inclusive does not apply when you precede it with "includes." That's the "plain meaning" of the word.

[25]   Freight train coming through! What's the one word that covers all these items?

[26]   How do you measure the tenant's desire? Perhaps when the Tenant takes steps to deal with it disadvantageously.

[27]   Start a new sentence here.

and be binding [28] upon the successors and assigns of the Landlord.

IN WITNESS WHEREOF the Corporation [29] has executed this consent as of [30] the 30th day of May 1987. [31]

---

[28]   You only need one verb here, "to bind." "This contract binds . . . ."

[29]   What Corporation? That is not a defined term. This contract is between Landlord and Tenant.

[30]   What is "as of" a date? Did they execute it on that date or not? If it is important then make sure it was done when it should have been done. If it is not, then just put the date on which it was signed and include an effective date clause.

[31]   May 30, 1987.

CONTRACT - REDRAFT INTO PLAIN ENGLISH

In this first redraft, I've simply tried to take the language used in the original agreement and simplify it. I've stuck with the same organization and included equivalents of all the clauses found in the original.

However, I don't that is going far enough, as you will see in my second rewrite.

AGREEMENT

BETWEEN:

ABC Real Estate Corporation

The "Landlord"

AND

Joe's Pizza, Limited

The "Tenant"

BACKGROUND [32]

1.   The Landlord owns a building at 123 Main Street, Toronto, Ontario.[33]

2.   In an agreement dated July 10, 1987 [34] (the "Agreement"), the Tenant leased premises in the building [35] (the "Leased Premises") from the Landlord. The lease was for the period specified in the Agreement ("Interim Period").

3.   The Agreement is subject to the terms of a written lease ("Written Lease"). The Written Lease is attached to the Agreement and labeled "Schedule C."

---

[32]   Notice that there is not a "Whereas" to be found in these recitals. Each element of the recitals is a separate sentence in a complete paragraph. If you are uncomfortable with this heading, "Recitals" is fine. One of my students also suggested "Agreed Facts."

[33]   This normal street address is sufficiently unambiguous.

[34]   This date merely identifies the agreement.

[35]   I still want a suite number or the like.

4.   The Tenant and Landlord have agreed to renew the lease[36] for five years from the end of the Interim Period.

5.   The Tenant has asked the Landlord to consent to a deed of trust and mortgage ("Trust Deed")[37] between the Tenant and ABC Trust Company ("Trust"). The Trust Deed is dated May 30, 1987.[38]

6.   The Trust Deed purports to give Trust priority over the Landlord's rights under the Agreement and the Written Lease.[39]

AGREEMENT

A.   The Landlord gives the Tenant its consent to encumber the Tenant's property which is on the Leased Premises and specified in the Trust Deed.[40] This consent is subject to Paragraph B, below. It is conditional on the Tenant providing the Landlord or its solicitors with a photocopy of the executed Trust Deed within two weeks of its execution.

---

[36]   Notice I don't say "on the same terms and conditions" since the idea of renewal means the same lease is continued for a new term.

[37]   Since this is the only trust deed mentioned, we don't really need to define it. It is completely unambiguous within the context of this document.

[38]   Again, this just identifies the trust deed.

[39]   I wouldn't define this as "Landlord's Rights." Why restrict which of the Landlord's rights are not limited by the Trust Deed. After all, you are presumably drafting this for the Landlord so why not make the language as all encompassing as possible? Admittedly, the court may give the phrase a restricted reading, buy why ask for that?

[40]   My original language here was " . . . Tenant's property on the Leased Premises as specified in the Trust Deed." That makes it confusing whether "as specified in the Trust Deed" modifies "property" or "premises." This makes it clear.

B.   The Landlord does not consent and in no circumstances shall be deemed[41] to consent to any provision of the Trust Deed which lessens the Landlord's rights. This includes the provision in Articles III, IV, VI, VII, VIII and IX of the Trust Deed. These purport to limit the Landlord's rights to:

    a.   disdrain for non payment of rent;

    b.   recover accelerated rent;

    c.   enforce a lien on all the tenant's property[42] in the event of the Tenant's default on the Agreement or Written Lease;

    d.   enforce any rights involving insurance;

    e.   re-enter and/or re-let the Leased Premises or avail itself of any other similar remedies in the event of the Tenant's default on the Agreement or Written Lease; or

    f.   recover from the Tenant any property owned by the Tenant and charged under the Trust Deed when the Tenant desires to deal with the property in a manner not to the Landlord's advantage.

---

[41]   Like all passive verbs this leaves open the question of just who is doing the deeming. Are you telling the court it can't deem? Can you do that? Do you want to? Or is the Tenant merely agreeing that it will not argue that the Landlord's actions should be used to construe is consent? By moving this to the active, you can clear up those issues. Also, this sentence can still be cut in two. The actual consent issue and the deemed consent issue are really separate.

[42]   This seems to cover the waterfront covered by the original series. If you think it doesn't what one word do you think would encompass all the ideas in the original list.

RULING LAW AND SUCCESSION

This consent is governed by the laws of the Province of Ontario. It binds the successors and assigns of the Landlord.

Date of Execution: May 30, 1987.

CONTRACT - COMPLETE REWRITE

In this rewrite, I have attempted to get to the core of the agreement. That means I've thrown out a large part of the recitals. They're just not relevant. I've also further simplified the language.

For examples of complicated documents written in simple language, get copies of the consumer documents CitiBank uses in New York. They're well written, clear and easy to understand.

CONSENT TO ENCUMBRANCE [43]

BETWEEN:

ABC Real Estate Corporation

The "Landlord"

AND

Joe's Pizza, Limited

The "Tenant"

INTRODUCTION

The tenant leases premises from the Landlord at Suite 111, 123 Main Street, Toronto, Ontario (the "Leased Premises").[44] In the lease, the Tenant has agreed not to encumber its title in its property in the Leased Premises if that encumbrance is detrimental to the interests of the Landlord. However, the Tenant may request and the Landlord may grant consent for such an encumbrance.

This document is that consent.

CONSENT

A.   The Landlord gives the Tenant its consent [45] to encumber the Tenant's property

---

[43]   This title makes it clear at a glance what this document is.

[44]   I don't think we really care how they got into their current landlord/tenant relationship. That they are is enough so that's all that belongs.

[45]   I've dropped the "subject to the conditions below" phrase because the document must be read as a whole.

in the Leased Premises. This consent is limited to the property specified in a trust deed [46] dated May 30, 1987, between the Tenant and ABC Trust Company.

B.   The Landlord does not consent to any provision of the trust deed which lessens the Landlord's rights. The Tenant agrees that no action of the Landlord shall be construed as deeming its consent. This includes [47] Articles III, IV, VI, VII, VIII and IX of the trust deed which purport to limit the Landlord's rights to:

a.   distrain for non-payment of rent;

b.   recover accelerated rent;

c.   enforce a lien on all property of the Tenant in the event of the Tenant's default on the lease;

d.   enforce any rights involving insurance;

e.   re-enter or re-let the Leased Premises or to avail itself of any other similar remedies in the event of the Tenant's default on the lease; or

f.   recover from the Tenant any of the Tenant's property charged under the trust deed if the

---

[46]   Note that I've not defined "Trust Deed" since this is the only one mentioned. Since this is the only trust deed ever mentioned, we don't need to define it as a term. It is completely unambiguous within the context of this document.

[47]   No "without restricting the generality of the forgoing" since that is what "includes" means.

Tenant attempts [48] to deal with the property in a way not to the Landlord's advantage.

C.   This consent is only effective if, within two weeks of its execution, the Tenant delivers a photocopy of the trust deed to the Landlord or to its solicitors.

RULING LAW AND SUCCESSION

This consent is governed by the laws of the Province of Ontario. This consent binds the successors and assigns of the Landlord.

Date of Execution: May 30, 1987. [49]

---

[48]   I like this better than "wishes." I can see an attempt. I cannot see a wish. If I can't see a wish, how can I reasonably act upon its occurrence?

[49]   One point of law. I hope this is to be executed under seal because there is no consideration for the landlord's promise. If it is to be under seal, I would recommend a paragraph saying, "This document is being executed 'under seal.' The parties acknowledge that a sealed contract is enforceable even if either party has received nothing in return for its promise." Without similar language, I suspect a good lawyer could break a contract under seal on the grounds that a little red dot printed on the document does not provide the formal notice it once did.

OPINION LETTER

GENERAL COMMENTS

This letter is to the committee that must decide
whether a person gets legal aid for an appeal. The
committee deals with as many as ten of these an hour
so the letter must be short, to the point and
persuasive.

Overall, this is not a bad first draft. It needs a rework
for better organization and the author has to make a
concerted effort to trim the use of legalese. But most
everything needed is here so this is not atypical of
what you might get coming out of your drafting time.
It's just a question of rewriting and trimming.

What Are You Trying To Accomplish?

This letter is to let the legal aid committee know why
you think of this case as a possible appeal case. The
committee's job is to decide whether the case merits
the expense of public money. They don't want to
know that it is a sure winner, just that it has a good
chance and raises important legal issues.

Who Is Your Audience?

The committee members do a lot of this. They are
professionals so you need to treat them that way: no
bafflegab, no b.s. Just give them the information they
need to know, including the downside of the case if
there is one. As I said, they see up to ten of these an
hour. They need fast, concise information. What is
the bottom line?

Overall Organization

This piece has a natural organization that the author seems to fight. Remember, all good writing has a beginning a middle and an end. The beginning here is a quick introduction to what this letter is for — its purpose — and the background that lets the committee members know the facts they need. In the middle come the two sections on the legal grounds for the appeals and finally a quick close. You'll notice that in the rewrite I've added section headings to make this organization clear.

The original version of the letter starts on the next page.

Bright, Red and Scooter

Barristers and Solicitors
123 Granville St.
Toronto, ONT M2T 2P3
(416) 555-1111

January 20, 1986

Dear sir: [1]

Re: John Terrence
Appeal to Court of Appeal
Provincial Certificate # 12345

Mr. Terrence seeks [2] to appeal against [3] his conviction for possession of stolen goods over [4] $200 contrary to [5] s. 312 of the Criminal Code and [6] against the sentence of 12 months imprisonment and one year probation. [7] Mr. Terrence was convicted in

---

[1] The author of this letter needs a new secretary. Both words of the salutation should be capitalized: Dear Sir.

[2] He "wishes" to appeal.

[3] " . . . . wishes to appeal his conviction . . . ." is fine. You don't need the "against."

[4] Over refers to physical position above something. The correct phrase here is "worth more than."

[5] This phrase ("contrary to") is a bit of legalese. Drop it. Just note the section number either in parentheses or between commas.

[6] Rather than trying to hang together one long sentence, start a new one here.

[7] Why does the author speak of "twelve months imprisonment" but "one year probation". Pick one or the other and be consistent.

Toronto by the Honourable[8] Judge Smith,[9] sitting without a jury, on January 23rd, 1986, and was sentenced January 24th, 1986. The trial consisted of one day of evidence on January 23rd and one hour[10] on January 24th. He is presently incarcerated[11] at the Metro West Detention Centre. The following opinion is based on a review of the Prisoner's Notice of Appeal and discussions with trial counsel.[12]

The facts of the offence may be briefly summarized as follows.[13] On January 29th,[14] 1984, Mr. Terrence, who was 19 years of age at the time,[15] was[16] a passenger in a stolen

---

Start a new paragraph here. The first paragraph is the introduction saying he wants to appeal. The second paragraph gives the history of this case.

[8] Not needed in a letter like this. In addressing a letter to Judge Smith, yes. Here, no.

[9] Does he or she have a first name? What is it?

[10] Was this one more hour of evidence or was it speaking to sentence? Is it important? Yes, because the author has left his reader confused.

[11] Legalese _ "serving his sentence."

[12] This last sentence does not belong in this paragraph. Put it in one of its own. Better yet, put it at the end of the letter.

[13] This sentence begins what I call the "Background" section in my rewrite. As it stands, it has several problems. First, " . . . may be briefly summarized . . . ." This verb is both conditional and passive. Who may briefly summarize the facts? Why "may"? Don't be afraid to state what you have to say positively. "Here are the facts of this case." Better yet, put a heading on the section, "Background" or "Facts of the Case" and then just tell them.

[14] Cardinal numbers are more normal in dates: January 29, 1984.

[15] "On January 29, 1984, Mr. Terrence, 19, was a passenger . . . ."

[16] The verb "was" is separated from its subject, "Mr. Terrence," by nine words. Pull the core of the sentence together by splitting this into two sentences.

Mr. Terrence was a passenger in a stolen car. He was 19 at the time.

motor vehicle.[17] This vehicle was being driven by Rich Hayes,[18] a friend of Mr. Terrence. Mr. Terrence testified that he did not know the car was stolen, but rather believed Rich Hayes had borrowed it from his brother-in-law. Mr. Hayes had borrowed a vehicle[19] from his brother-in-law on previous occasions[20] and Mr. Hayes told Mr. Terrence that it was his brother-in-law's new car. While travelling on Highway 401 the vehicle was stopped by the police after a short chase. Mr. Terrence ran from the scene but was found hiding under some bushes. Mr. Terrence testified that he ran away because he was in possession of a small quantity of hashish, which he wished to hide. No evidence was led at trial as to whether or not Mr. Terrence gave a statement to the police when he was apprehended. In his reasons for judgment, Judge Smith rejected the testimony of Mr. Terrence and found that Mr. Terrence knew that the vehicle was stolen and that he was in possession of the vehicle by virtue of s. 3(4)(b) of the Criminal Code which provides as follows:

(b) where one of two or more persons, with the knowledge and consent of the rest, has anything in his custody or possession, it shall be deemed to be in the custody and possession of each and all of them.

In my respectful [21] opinion, the Honourable [22] Judge Smith made several [23] errors which could

---

17 A car? A truck? A motorcycle? A moped? A red, 1965 Mustang convertible?

18 Passive. "Mr. Terrence's friend, Rich Hayes, was driving the car."

19 Car.

20 Before

21 In *my* respectful opinion, this particular chestnut can be retired. You show respect for the court _ or the committee or other lawyers or your clients _ by not wasting their time with

constitute valid grounds for appeal.[24]   These
are set out below: [25]

1. Possession

The evidence does not show that Mr.
Terrence had any control over the
vehicle. While s. 3(4)(b) of the
Criminal Code refers only to knowledge
and consent on the part of the accused,
case law, from Ontario and other
provinces,[26] has made it clear that the
Crown must prove that the accused had
some control over the property involved.
See: R. v. Colvin and Gladue (1942), 78
CCC 282 (BCCA) and R. v. Lou Hay Hung
(1946), 85 CCC 308 (Ont CA).

2. Adverse Influence

The trial Judge also erred in drawing an
adverse inference from the failure of Mr.
Terrence to give his explanation to the
police officers. It is well
established [27] that no adverse inference
can be drawn [28] from the failure to give

---

obsequiousness. You show respect by being respectful, not by
saying you're being respectful.

[22]   Again, not needed in this type of letter.

[23]   There may be "several errors" but this letter is about two. Use
of a general word like several tells me the author has not
thought out the argument in advance.

[24]   This sentence starts an entirely new section of the letter and
should be preceded by some kind of flag or transition such as
a heading like "Grounds for Appeal."

[25]   If they are set out below, the reader can see that. If they are
not, saying so won't make it so. This sentence is completely
unnecessary. Just drop it.

[26]   This is obvious from the citations so why say it here?

[27]   By whom? "The law is clear that . . . " or "The cases make it
clear that . . . ."

[28]   Two points. No adverse inference *may* be drawn. Certainly
one *can* be drawn. That's why we have the rule saying you
may not. Second, again this is a passive verb leaving open the
question of who can (or may) not draw an adverse inference.

an explanation after an accused had been arrested and cautioned the he need not make any statement. See: R.v. Hawke (1975), 22 CCC (2d) 19 (Ont CA). In any event, there was no evidence as to whether or not Mr. Terrence gave any explanation.[29]

While certain other findings made by the trial Judge were essentially findings of fact based on the judge's assessment of credibility,[30] In my opinion [31] the errors set out above [32] are of sufficient importance [33] that there is a reasonable likelihood of success on an appeal against conviction.[34]

Mr. Terrence also seeks to appeal against [35] the sentence of 12 months imprisonment.[36] Mr. Terrence was born on January 5, 1966 and

---

Try this: "A trier of fact may not draw an adverse inference . . . ."

[29] The most serious problem here is that there is nothing in the letter that shows the judge drew any inference from the lack of testimony. You need something to back this up. How about a short quote from the judge's opinion.

Even if it was OK to draw an inference from failure to make a statement, in this case there is no evidence at all, one way or the other. That could be an important point and should be emphasized.

[30] And? The other findings of the trial judge are irrelevant. They're not the grounds for appeal so why mention them. Leave them out.

[31] "I believe"

[32] "these errors"

[33] Replace "of sufficient importance" with "enough."

[34] ". . . that an appeal is reasonably likely to succeed."

[35] ". . . . wishes to appeal . . . ."

[36] "one year in jail" Also, this sentence starts a new topic and should have a new heading.

is therefore 20 years of age.[37] He has the following prior criminal record.

Jan. 6, 1982, Toronto	Theft under $200	Absolute Discharge
March 1, 1982, Toronto	Theft under $200	Conditional Discharge, 6 months probation
Sept. 1, 1982 Toronto	Theft under $200 (two counts); failure to appear	Suspended Sentence, nine months probation (both counts); 15 days gaol.[38]
July 6, 1983 Toronto	Break, enter and theft; breach of probation	60 days gaol and two years probation; 15 days gaol consecutive

At the time of this offence, Mr. Terrence was living with his mother, his parents having separated approximately one year prior to the offence.[39] However, his parents have now reconciled[40] and are supportive[41] of Mr. Terrence. Mr. Terrence has a grade 9 education and at present[42] is unemployed.[43]

---

[37] I fail to see the connection between his wish to appeal, his age and his criminal record. Start a new paragraph with this sentence. And either give his birthday or his age but not both.

[38] I'll bet money you had to look "gaol" up the first time you saw it. Just because the *Criminal Code*, which was drafted in the 1880s (for India, by the way but they didn't want it), uses the word "gaol" doesn't mean that the rest of us have to continue to do so. Today, the spelling is *jail*. Or do you still spell "show" "shew"?

[39] Two ideas here. Give each its own sentence. "At the time of this offence, Mr. Terrence was living with his mother. His parents had separated a year previously."

[40] " . . . . Are now back together . . . ."

[41] Verb turned into an adjective, this time. His parents "support" him.

[42] "is at present" is redundant. "Is" is in the present tense. It means right now. So you don't need to say so unless you are trying to make a big point of it.

He is currently[44] enrolled in a Manpower retraining course to begin[45] on March 1st, 1986. If legal aid is granted for this appeal, then an application for bail will be made[46] to enable Mr. Terrence to[47] take this course.

In my opinion, an appeal against sentence has a reasonable chance of success, having regard to a number of factors.[48] Although Mr. Terrence has a relatively lengthy criminal record, the longest sentence previously imposed was a total of 75 days imprisonment. Imposition of a sentence of 12 months imprisonments for a relatively minor offence in my opinion[49] is unduly harsh and in violation of[50] the "jump" principle. See: Ruby, _Sentencing_, Second Edition (Toronto: Butterworths, 1980) p. 102. Further, the trial judge erred in principle

---

[43] Start a new paragraph with this sentence. The previous paragraph was speaking of his home situation. This one is about his education and employment prospects.

[44] "Is currently" is like "is at present." Just "is."

[45] "which begins"

[46] By whom? Again, a passive verb leaving open the question who is going to apply. "Mr. Terrence will apply for bail . . . ."

[47] "so that Mr. Terrence can"

[48] Again, the author waffles on the number of grounds of appeal by saying "several factors." Again, there are two.

Also, this paragraph serves the same kind of function as the sections the author previously indented and put under the headings "Possession" and "Adverse Inference." This is a parallel function so the author should use a parallel construction including headings and indents.

[49] Is your opinion about the sentence or about the severity of the offence. Take this kind of superfluousness out of the core of your sentence and it will work a lot better.

> In my opinion, imposition of a twelve month sentence for a minor offence is unduly harsh and violates the "jump" principle."

[50] Verb turned into a noun. "The sentence . . . violates the 'jump' principle."

in refusing to order a pre-sentence report. Mr. Terrence was relatively young and such a report could have given the Judge a clearer picture of Mr. Terrence's situation. Prior to the appeal, an application could be made to a Judge of the Court of Appeal for the post-sentence report.

I trust this is the information which the committee [51] requires but should you require any further information or material please contact me.

Yours truly, [52]

---

[51] If you are writing to the committee, they are "you," not "the committee."

[52] In a complementary close, both words are capitalized: Yours Truly.

OPINION LETTER REWRITE

In rewriting the opinion letter, I've tried to clarify and make it a lot easier for the committee members to read. I've shortened the sentences, added headings and used simpler words. I liked the basic organization and kept it.

Bright, Red and Scooter

Barristers and Solicitors

123 Granville St.
Toronto, ONT M2T 2P3
(416) 555-1111

January 31, 1986

Committee Members:

Re: John Terrence
Appeal to Court of Appeal
Provincial Certificate # 12345

John Terrence wishes to appeal his conviction for possession of stolen goods worth more than $200 (Criminal Code s. 312). He also wishes to appeal his sentence of a year in jail and a year probation.

BACKGROUND

Mr. Terrence was arrested following a short police chase of a stolen car on January 29, 1985. He was 19 at the time. He testified at his trial that he thought the car belonged to the brother-in-law of the driver, Rich Hayes. Mr. Terrence had previously gone riding in a car lent to Mr. Hayes by his brother-in-law. He testified that Mr. Hayes told him the car was his brother-in-law's new car.

When police stopped the car, Mr. Terrence ran from the scene. He was arrested a short distance away, hiding under bushes. He testified that he was trying to hide a small quantity of hashish.

The Crown led no evidence at trial as to whether Mr. Terrence gave police a statement at the time of his arrest.

The trial started January 23, 1986, and ran over for one hour on the 24th. Judge John Smith, sitting without a jury, rejected Mr. Terrence's testimony and found that he knew that the car was stolen. He held that Mr. Terrence was "in possession" of the car under s. 3(4)(b) of the <u>Criminal Code</u> which says,

> "Where one of two or more persons, with the knowledge and consent of the rest, has anything in his custody or possession, it shall be deemed to be in the custody and possession of each and all of them."

Judge Smith sentenced Mr. Terrence on January 24 without a pre-sentence report. Mr. Terrence is currently serving his sentence at the Metro West Detention Centre.

At the time of his arrest, Mr. Terrence was living with his mother. His parents, then separated, are back together and support their son.

He has a grade nine education and no job, but he is enrolled in a Manpower retraining program set to begin on March 1, 1986. If you grant legal aid assistance for this appeal, Mr. Terrence will be applying for bail so he can take this course.

<u>APPEAL OF CONVICTION</u>

In my opinion, Judge Smith made two errors that could constitute grounds for an appeal of the conviction.

1. <u>Possession</u>

   The evidence does not show that Mr.
   Terrence had any control over the car.
   While s. 3(4)(b) of the <u>Criminal Code</u>
   speaks only of possession, case law makes
   it clear that the Crown must prove some
   control over the property involved. See:
   <u>R</u>. v. <u>Colvin and Gladue</u> (1942), 78 CCC
   282 (BCCA) and <u>R</u>. v. <u>Lou Hay Hung</u> (1946),
   85 CCC 308 (Ont CA).

2. <u>Adverse Inference</u>

   The trial judge apparently drew an
   adverse inference from the failure of Mr.
   Terrence to give his explanation to
   police officers. This was an error for
   two reasons. First, there was no
   evidence one way or the other as to
   whether Mr. Terrence gave a statement to
   police. Second, even if he didn't, cases
   such as <u>R</u>. v. <u>Hawke</u> (1975), 22 CCC (2d)
   19 (Ont CA), make it clear that a trier
   of fact may not draw an adverse inference
   from the failure of an accused to give an
   explanation after he has been arrested
   and cautioned that he need not make a
   statement.

I believe these errors are sufficient to
give an appeal of the conviction a
reasonable chance of success.

<u>APPEAL OF SENTENCE</u>

Mr. Terrence also wish to appeal his
sentence.

He has a record of seven convictions prior
to this case.

Jan. 6, 1982, Toronto	Theft under $200	Absolute Discharge
March 1, 1982, Toronto	Theft under $200	Conditional Discharge, 6 months probation
Sept. 1, 1982 Toronto	Theft under $200 (two counts); failure to appear	Suspended Sentence, nine months probation (both counts); 15 days jail.
July 6, 1983 Toronto	Break, enter and theft; breach of probation	60 days jail and two years probation; 15 days jail consecutive

Two factors particularly argue for a successful appeal of sentence.

1. <u>Harsh and Violates Jump Principle</u>

Though he has a relatively long criminal record, the longest sentence he has previously received was a total of 75 days. I believe the year long term in this case is unduly harsh and violates the "jump" principal outlined by Clayton Ruby in his book <u>Sentencing</u> (2nd ed., Butterworths, Toronto, 1980, p. 102).

2. <u>No Pre-Sentence Report</u>

The trial judge should have ordered a pre-sentence report. At 20, Mr. Terrence is still relatively young and a pre-sentence report might have given the judge a better picture. (Prior to an appeal, Mr. Terrence could apply to a judge of the Court of Appeal for a post-sentence report.)

I believe an appeal of sentence has a good chance of succeeding.

BASIS OF OPINION

The information in this opinion letter is based on a review of the Prisoner's Notice of Appeal and talks with Mr. Terrence's trial counsel. I hope it is what you need to make your decision. If you need more or if I can help in any other way, please call on me.

Yours Truly,

BIBLIOGRAPHY

This is not meant to be a complete bibliography either on the subject of legal writing or the on the writing process. These are just some articles and books that I have found useful and interesting. Many of them are already cited earlier in the book but I thought you might find it convenient to have them all in one place.

Books

Benson, Herbert, and Miriam Klipper, *The Relaxation Response*, Harper Paperbacks, New York, 2000.

Brand, Norman, and John O. White, *Legal Writing; The Strategy of Persuasion*, St. Martin's Press, New York, 1994.

Blake, Marion, *Plain Language and the Law: An Inquiry and Bibliography*, report no. 4 in the series "Access to Justice: Research Reports on Public Legal Education and Information," Department of Justice, Canada, March 1986.

Coe, Richard, *Process, Form and Substance: An Advanced Rhetoric*, 2nd ed., John Wiley & Sons, New York, 1981.

Cowan, Gregory and Elizabeth Cowan, *Writing*, Scott Foresman and Company, 1980, p. 34.

de Bono, Edward, *Six Thinking Hats*, Penguin Books, 2000.

Dernbach, John C., and Richard V. Singleton II, *A Practical Guide to Legal Writing and Legal Method*, 2nd ed., Fred B. Rothman, Littleton, CO, 2009.

Elbow, Peter, *Writing With Power: Techniques for Mastering the Writing Process*, Oxford University Press, New York, 1998.

Ellsworth, Blanche and John A. Higgins, *English Simplified* (12th ed.), Longman, 2009

Ghiselin, Brewster, *The Creative Process*, Transformational Book Circle, 2005.

Gordon, Karen Elizabeth, *The Deluxe Transitive Vampire: A Handbook of Grammar for the Innocent, the Eager and the Doomed*, Pantheon Books, New York, 1993.

Gordon, Karen Elizabeth, *The Well-Tempered Sentence: A Punctuation Handbook for the Innocent, the Eager and the Doomed*, Mariner Books, 2003.

Lindemann, Erica and Daniel Anderson, *A Rhetoric for Writing –Teachers,* 4th ed., Oxford University Press, 2nd Edition, 2001.

Mellinkoff, David, *Legal Writing: Sense and Nonsense*, West, 1982.

Mellinkoff, David, *The Language of the Law,* Wipf & Stock, 2004.

Rico, Gabriele Lusser, *Writing the Natural Way, J.P. Tarcher*, Inc., Los Angeles, 2000.

Articles

Bablitch, William A, "Writing to Win," The Compleat Lawyer, Winter 1988.

Benson, Robert W., "Legalese v. Plain English: An Empirical Study of Persuasion and Credibility in Appellate Brief Writing," 20 Loyola of Los Angeles Law Review 301, January 1987.

Benson, Robert W., "Plain English Comes to Court," Litigation, Volume 13, Number 1, Fall 1986.

Benson, Robert W., "The End of Legalese: The Game is Over," XIII Review of Law and Social Change 519.

Christensen, Francis, "A Generative Rhetoric of the Paragraph" in *Contemporary Rhetoric, Conceptual Background With Readings*, Harcourt Brace Jovanovich, 1975.

Christensen, Francis, "A Generative Rhetoric of the Sentence" in *Contemporary Rhetoric, Conceptual Background With Readings*, Harcourt Brace Jovanovich, 1975.

Edgerton, Thomas Selden, "After Seven Centuries, the True Meaning of SS," Michigan Bar Journal, January 1986, p 94.

Fadem, Jerrold, "Legalese as Legal Does: Lawyers Clean Up Their Act," Prosecutor's Brief 14 (Jan-Feb 1979).

Galbraith, John Kenneth, "Writing, Typing and Economics," The Atlantic Monthly, March 1978.

Smith, Robert B., "Eschew Obfuscation or How Not to Sound Like a Lawyer," Bar Leader, March-April 1986, p. 20.

Stark, Steven, "Why Lawyers Can't Write," Bar Leader, Volume 10, Number 6, May-June 1985, pg 15.

Canadian Law Information Council

The Canadian Law Information Council has some good material on plain language legal writing. Most of their material is available on loan. Write them or call for more information on what they have.

Canadian Law Information Council
2409 Yonge Street
Toronto, ONT
M4P 2E7
(416) 483-3802

SPELLING RULES YOU SHOULD KNOW

1. **q** is always written as **qu.** It never stands alone in English words. Examples are queen, quick, quarrel. Note that some foreign words do us Q on it's own as in Qatar.

2. No English word ends is **v** or **j**.

3. Plurals:

    a) Regular plurals are made by adding **s**, for example, dogs, cats, cars.

    b) Plurals of words with endings that hiss (**s, x, z, sh** and **ch**) are formed by adding **es.** Examples are passes, boxes, buzzes, washes, and churches.

    c) Words ending in **o** preceded by a consonant are made plural by adding **es**. Examples: potatoes, volcanoes. **Exceptions:** pianos, solos, Eskimos.

    d) Nouns that end in **f** change it to a **v** then add **es** to form the plural form. Examples: leaves, wolves.

4. Use **ck** to give a **k** sound when it follows a short vowel (a vowel that is not pronounced with its name) or at the end of a syllable or root word. Examples, pick, wreckage, track, jack, rocket.

5. One syllable words ending in a single vowel followed by a single consonant double the consonant before adding endings. Examples are stop, stopped, stopping; flat, flatter, flatten; swim, swimming, swimmer. **Exceptions:** words that end in **x** because a terminal **x** sounds as a **ks** and so is treated as a double consonant: fixing, boxing, foxy.

6. In counties tending toward British spelling (Britain, Canada, Australia and New Zealand) words ending in a single **l** after a single vowel double the **l** before adding a suffix (traveller, cancelled, signalling, metallic). In the United States, the simpler single **l** is often used (counselor).

7. If a word

    a)   has more than one syllable,

    b)   ends is a **t** preceeded by a vowel, and

    c)   has the accent on the final syllable,

    *then d*ouble the final **t** when adding suffixes. (permit?permitted, regret?regretted. However, visit?visited and benefit?benefited (both exceptions have the accent not on the last syllable.

8. If a word ends in **e**,

    a)   drop the **e** before adding a suffix the starts with a vowel (lovable, gracing) but

    b)   keep the **e** if the suffix begins with a consonant (lovely, graceful)

9. "All" and "well" when combined into words with another syllable lose their second **l**. (Already, welcome, although)

10. "Full" and "till" when used as a suffix drop the second **l**. (joyful, cheerful, until)

11. The sound **ee** at the end of a word is almost always a **y**. (Sorry, hurry, Kentucky). Exceptions are some words derived from other languages (macaroni, vermicelli, taxi) and the words committee and coffee.

12. If a word ends in a consonant followed by **y**, change the **y** to **i** before adding any ending except **–ing** (party?parties; heavy?heaviness; funny?funniness but cry?crying).

13. **C** followed by **e**, **i**, or **y** has an **s** sound (centre, ceiling); otherwise it sounds as **k** (circle, cycle, cave).

14. Except at the beginning of a word (Ship, shore), the sound **sh** is almost always spelled **ti**, **ci** or **si** (national, infectious, ancient, gracious, musician). **Exception: ship** when used as a suffix as in worship.)

15. **I** comes before **e** and are pronounced as **ee** (brief, field, priest) **except:**

     a)   when they are pronounced as **a** (neighbor, weigh) or

     b)   they follow the letter **c** (conceive, ceiling).

16. An **e** on the end of the word makes the previous vowel long (pronounced as its own name) as in hate, ride, cube, bake. **Exceptions:** done, come, some, give, have.

17. **W** before **or** is often pronounced **wer** (worship, worst, work).

18. **Its** is the possessive form of **it** (*Its meaning is clear.*) **It's** is the conjunction of **it is** (*It's going to be a nice day.*)

19. **There** refers to a place (*It's over there.*). **Their** is the possessive form of **they** (*Their* car is over there.)

COPYRIGHT ACKNOWLEDGEMENTS

Mr. Justice M.R. Taylor and the Continuing Legal Education Society of British Columbia for "Effective Legal Writing for Understanding, Clarity and Precision."